Financing Your Next BILLION$$$

Know Your Impact, Stand Out from The Crowd and Get Funded

YVONNE E. GAMBLE

Copyright © 2020 Yvonne E. Gamble

All rights reserved.

ISBN: 9781717727282
Independently published

CONTENTS

DEDICATION 1

PREFACE 2

ACKNOWLEDGMENTS 6

INTRODUCTION 7

CHAPTER 1 ASSESSING YOUR CAPITAL RAISE 9
Does My Business Fit the VC Model? - Capital Raise - 5 Benefits of Having Venture Capital Investment - Is VC Right For Me? - Navigating the Shark Tank? - VC A Different Breed - What VC's Thrive On - Welcome to the World of VC's - The VC Landscape - The VC Equity Position - VC Competition

CHAPTER 2 WHO IS ON YOUR TEAM? 18
Build a Great Team - Who is on Your Team - Finding the Right Co-Founder - Boards - Shareholders

CHAPTER 3 WHICH WAY TO YOUR MARKET 24
Product Development - Lean Startup Methodology - Product Development Cycle Explained - Design Thinking - Your Competition - Manage Political and Regulatory Risk - Multi-Stakeholder Action Needed - Understanding Market Risk - Your Value Promise - 6 STEPS To Target Market

CHAPTER 4 SCALABILITY, AGILITY, ADAPTABILITY 33
Growth - Capitalization - Capitalization Table - Simplify The CAP Table

CHAPTER 5 LEGAL BASICS 38
Legal Basics - Intellectual Property - The Importance of Intellectual Property Asset Management - Exclusive Rights, Economic Value - Security of Intellectual Property - Viral Free Software A Worry For Tech Investors - VC Financing Documents

CHAPTER 6 KNOW YOUR INVESTOR 45
Into The Mind of The Equity Investor

CHAPTER 7 THE RIGHT PITCH 49
De-risking Your Startup - How to Prepare an Investor Pitch Deck - The Pitch Deck, The Presentation, AirBNB Pitch Deck

CHAPTER 8 HOW DEEP IS DUE DILIGENCE 55
What Level of Due Diligence Should I Expect? - Market and Competition - Supporting Data for Your Market Size - Detailed Analysis of Competitors

CHAPTER 9 DUE DILIGENCE REQUIRED INFORMATION……………..............…..60
H1 Required Due Diligence - Online Application

CHAPTER 10 60 MINUTES WITH AN INVESTOR…………………….......................66
60 Minutes With an Investor - Open With 3 Slides, Present A Full Story - 10 Steps to Assure a Successful Capital Raise

CHAPTER 11 BREAKING DOWN BARRIERS TO FUNDING…………………..........70
6 things Billionaires do Differently - How MONEY is Made - What is your Relationship with Money? - The Strength of Money

CHAPTER 12 DOMINATE THE DECADE……………………………………….........78
3 Strategies Business Owners Can Implement Now - Global Fundraising Principles Every Business Must Know - 3 Ways to Dominate the Decade - Building A Humanitarian Investment Ecosystem - The business case for companies to engage in humanitarian response

REFERENCES ……...96

ABOUT THE AUTHOR...98

DEDICATION

To my family, Fredrick, Giovanna, and Erika for their never ending support and encouragement it always warmed my heart and kept me going.

PREFACE

Everything you learn here will be from the Venture Capitalist's (VC) perspective. After preparing and presenting over 2500 one-page teasers for my clients I have learned what VC's want to see and what they do not want to see. Financing Your Next Billion$$$ will give you a glimpse into their world, so that you come away with a fuller understanding of whom you are polling out to in hopes of securing a willing, capable and amenable financial partner.

Financing Your Next Billion$$$ will be your guide to approaching, engaging and communicating your value to VCs that will get you to "YES we will fund your project".

Trust me; capital raising is very much like rocket science. Without proper guidance, planning and preparation it is easier for NASA to land a Rover on Mars than to successfully pitch to a VC that ends in funding. Not one time did NASA not land successfully on Mars since it began sending spacecraft to Mars in 1965. Each time a craft successfully launched, it successfully landed and begin sending telemetry complete with pictures, landscapes and topology. Now with more sophisticated cameras and seismic ability we can see water, which is an indication of life.

How did NASA propel a target at a moving object that orbits the sun in 687 days, at speeds of 53,700 miles per hour, with a rotation of only about 40 minutes slower than Earth, and varying distances based on the time of year? The minimum distance from the Earth to Mars is about 54.6 million kilometers (km). The farthest apart they can be is about 401 million km. The average distance apart at optimum time to launch is about 225 million km. After factoring in additional data for sub-space variances, gravitational force, NASA has been able to land successfully every time they launched. Probably does not sounds like your last VC pitch. You gave many details, but your audience did not really grasp what it had to do with them. Sometimes VCs become like deer staring at headlights and you are not sure if your project or your presentation has a chance of living.

By now, you are asking yourself what landing a Rover on Mars successfully has to do with a VC saying yes to your project. I am glad you asked! The answer is everything.

Simplify the process, talk to the right people, give them what they are looking for, factor in your constants, and make allowances for your variables; the result will be the probability for your success.

Your VC Success Calculator: CONSTANTS – VARIABLES = PROBABILITY OF SUCCESS.

To hit a moving target such as a planet, you have to know how it moves, where it will be at the time you want to get there. You must know its orbital cycles, its velocity, its gravitational force among other constants and variables. To simplify our model, we will keep to these three areas.

1. Orbital Cycle – A planet has three orbital cycles. The first is it spins on its axis. The second is its orbiting moon. The third is its orbit around the sun. All three of these cycles move simultaneously, independently and in conjunction with one another.
    a. A VC has three orbital cycles: they receive funds, they give debt or equity, and they receive revenue. To gain a deeper understanding of how a VC funds projects you must research your prospective VC's two primary layers.
    b. Layer one – The accumulation of funds for equity and debt funding.
    c. Layer two – The types of product/services that are of interest. Where does a VC want to invest their money and where do they want to spend their time?
    d. NOTE: While you are thinking of how your product/service will revolutionize the world, your project will have a chance of funding if you deliberately speak to the wants and desires of your potential benefactor.
    e. VC's host numerous expos, symposiums, forums and webinars as they scourge through business proposals looking for the next "BIG". Through these communications, they tell you exactly how to approach them, what they are looking for, and their investment cycles.
    f. Not understanding the VC's orbital cycles will have you pitching to the wrong team, at the wrong time, and with the wrong products/services.
2. Planet's Velocity – "The average distance of the Earth from sun is 93.5 million miles. This means that in 365.25 days the Earth travels 587.5 million miles. This works out to about 67 thousand miles per hour. This is the speed we travel 24 hours a day, 365.25 days a year. To appreciate the true meaning of velocity let us look at that of a few other planets: Mercury's orbital speed is $1.607(67,000)$ $=107.7$ thousand miles per hour, as befits a planet named for the god of speed. Mars is a bit of a laggard. Its speed is only $0.802(67,000) = 53.7$ thousand miles per hour. Pluto is veritably creeping around its orbit at only 10.7 thousand miles per hour, taking 248 years to complete its 5.9-billion-mile orbit of the sun.

1. A VCs velocity quotient is also measurable. Its sun being the center of where it is going, which determines the distance that we equate to time. Time to reach its apex [goal] is relative to hours [the actual # of hours that can be spent on a project in a day], which are relative to days, which are relative to years.
2. Most early to mid-term business owners today want their projects funded when they finish school, a course or a training, when they quit their jobs, close an existing business and are ready to begin a new venture.
3. Experienced business owners plan for at least 6 months to 1-year for venture capital infusion.
4. Seasoned business owners have learned that the timeline is not theirs and it belongs to the VC. They know that to achieve success they must align themselves with the VCs goals and mission plan. They must build a relationship that correlates to the VCs time, hours, days and years they want to spend on the project or service. Rover lands successfully on Mars every time, because it aligns with Mars' velocity.

3. Gravitational Force – The gravitational force of a planet can affect the atmosphere, climate and biometric movement of the planet, and any other planet in its gravitational path. Planets do not have to be in close proximity to one another to have an effect; they essentially have to be in line of sight, which for a planet is a very large sphere. There spheres of gravitational force can range from millions to trillions of miles away depending on the size of the planet. The exertion of the force has a change effect on planetary conditions, movement of planets, orbits of planets, growth, ocean currents and tremendous effect on living things on the planet.
    a. A VC's gravitonic effect is its sphere of influence over change. Based on what VC's invest in determines the course and outcomes of the next "BIG". When asked about the rise and fall of the Dotcoms' many will say that for VC's it was a disastrous losing proposition. However, every VC's knows exactly what it was, it was a "Change Methodology".
    b. Prior to the Dot.com era standards did not exist for online purchasing, social media, content news, cyber security, Bluetooth, syncing of data, BIG Data, Cloud storage, secure online banking and AI, just to name a few.
    c. Close your eyes and try to imagine your life without any one of these few items and the thousands of other Dot.com creations that exist today. Unimaginable, right?
    d. "Without failure, we can never move forward. The reason is that we do not know what we cannot do; therefore, having not failed, we would not know what we could do".

Make "Financing Your NEXT Billion$$$" your capital raise guide tool. Return to it often and you will net high returns on your capital raise.

Happy Capital Hunting,

Yvonne E. Gamble

ACKNOWLEDGMENTS

I would like to express my deepest appreciation to my spiritual leader, public relations media expert and dearest friend Baylan Megino who has the attitude and the substance of a spiritual genius; she continually and convincingly conveyed a spirt of "can do" what are you going to do" and "just breathe" throughout this project. Without her guidance and persistent help, the bringing forth and letting go of this work would not have been possible.

I would like to thank my staff members Yvonne Ranson Vice President Human Resources and Gwendolyn Hinton Vice President Finance & Client Services whose dedication demonstrated to me that concern for global affairs supported by an engagement in financial literacy should always transcend profit margins and provide a quest for our times.

In addition, I would like to give a sincere post humus thank you to Edward Bogetz, former Senior Vice President of Million Dollar banking adjustment department at American National Bank, Chicago, IL for believing in a recently graduated high school senior by affording me the opportunity and exposure to the world of million-dollar banking.

INTRODUCTION

Financing Your Next Billion$$$, the book, is the pebble that is dropped in a distant pond, that feeds into a lake that supplies fresh water to a river whose end dumps into a gulf that meets an ocean. Setting in motion a ripple effect that moves across the seas of the world as it ignites tidal waves of knowledge throughout the earth; and crescendo's into a tsunami upon a faraway shore – never asking permission, rather embolden its way through commandeering the water ways, ripping the land cleansing it of age old wood, disease and pestilence.

Please read this book with hopeful anticipation of what you will take away. This book is specifically designed to enhance your knowledge and understanding of why, when, where and how to finance your next billion.

FINANCING YOUR NEXT BILLION$$$

CHAPTER 1

ASSESSING YOUR CAPITAL RAISE

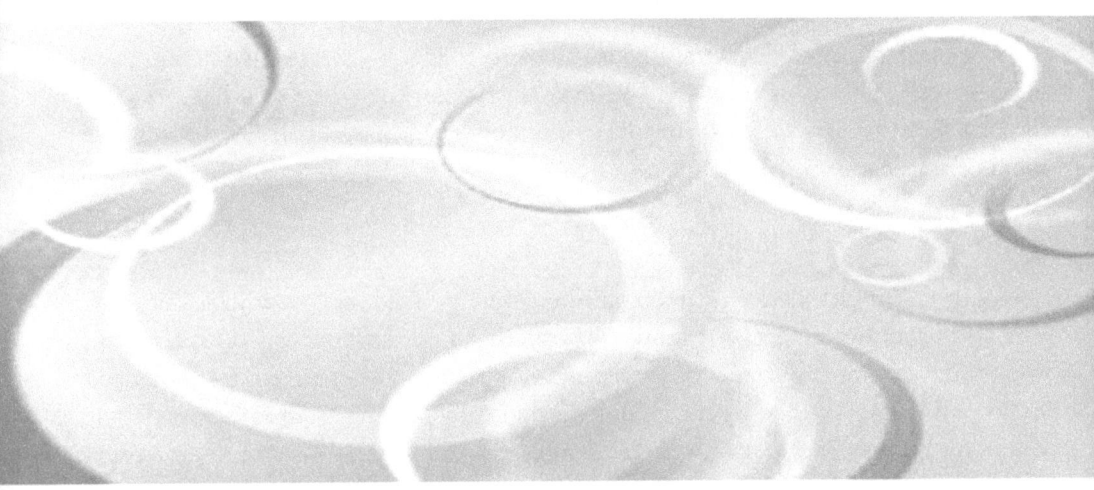

Does My Business Fit the VC MODEL?

While there are numerous financing options, there is no one size fits all or most. Where your company currently stands financially and its business credibility will be determining factors in which options are available to you. In this excerpt, we will look at just one aspect of financing your business and that is though venture capital (VC).

CAPITAL RAISE

Venture capital is the process of raising money from individuals and firms that invest in high growth, high risk companies. To compensate for higher risk, venture capital investors (VCs) expect a large return on their investment, higher than say a bank would expect. In addition, in exchange for their investment, VCs get partial ownership in your company, called equity, and some measure of control over decision-making.

Raising venture capital is a tough endeavor and is not right for all companies.

However, if you are considering this route for raising money, read on to learn the answers to the questions you have about why you are not attracting money. "Financing Your NEXT Billion$$$" will tell you everything you need to know about how to raise venture capital funding.

"To successfully raise venture capital, you're going to need a stellar operating business plan, investor business plan and a killer pitch deck."

5 BENEFITS OF HAVING VENTURE CAPITAL INVESTORS

You need money for any startup idea to come to life. Businesses that do not have the cash or assets to finance their business dream on their own will have to find funding from other resources. Acquiring investors is an option you should consider as this brings exponential advantages.

1. VC's provide funding

With the money that investments bring, you can build and grow your business. You will have the finances for marketing, overhead costs, shop or workspace rent, website development, product or service development, and other resources you need so you can increase your revenue. Also, having cash coming from investors means you don't have to use your own savings or touch your own assets and reserve them instead for when you need emergency funds.

2. VC's can contribute ideas and give advice

People or companies who invest in your startup will obviously hope to acquire profitable returns. With that in mind, business investors generally share their expertise with the entrepreneurs they are helping. They also contribute ideas for business growth or suggest solutions for challenges you come across. Some investors are business owners, lawyers, accountants, or finance professionals, so they have a wealth of knowledge and experience.

3. VC's bring connections

One of the most important ingredients to succeeding as an entrepreneur is gaining connections and building your network. When you are new to the industry, this will take some time and come with many challenges. Investors have partners and contacts of their own, and they can share these with you so you have more resources and connections to help build and grow your business.

4. VC's can give motivation

Startups face their own share of challenges, and sometimes it can get so overwhelming that you might just want to give up. But if you have investors who are banking on your success as much as you are, you will have people to encourage you and help you overcome the problems. They can motivate you to find solutions and work your way back towards the right path.

5. VC's can improve your business image

When a startup acquires investors, it means that there are people who see potential in your business and in your vision and are even willing to trust you with their own money. This can boost your image and even attract more investors or partners.

IS VC RIGHT FOR ME?

The first step in raising venture capital (VC) is making sure venture capital is right for your business. For many businesses and business owners, it is not. Here are some questions you should ask yourself to assess if you are a good fit.

Am I willing to give up some control of my business?

Many businesses owners underestimate the fact that raising venture capital means selling part of your company (i.e. equity) to sophisticated investors. Most business owners are used to being able to call all of the shots. Raising venture capital means being answerable to other people. You will need to have a plan that makes sense to your new partners. You will need to report monthly results to investors. In addition, you will have to answer to others if you fall short of company goals. It is possible you will lose control of your company depending on how your capital raise is structured and how well you perform.

Note: in order to raise venture capital and have the ability to issue equity shares, you will need to organize as a C-Corporation.

Navigating the Shark Tank

At the first mention of VC immediately images of polished boardrooms with long desks and eyes peering, twinkling with attack ready hands tightening around your throat and long sharp teeth poised to devour you as the first sign of sweat drips across your brow. You clear your throat and begin, wondering, "What have I gotten myself into".

You can swim with sharks and never suffer a bite. You just have to know which sharks, when to swim, where to swim and most importantly how to swim. If you do not know, it is best not to get in the deep water without an experienced guide.

VC's are "not all" like the description above, although bad press and TV shows like "Shark Tank", do not make it seem any better. While there are those that exist on greed and indifference, most follow a strict code of ethics to 'do no harm'.

VC's are very good people who have taken it upon themselves to bear the frontal brunt of the risk to allow you to realize your purpose and passions. They sink trillions into buying monetized instruments, holding them until they can comfortably release funds into a business without themselves going broke. The interest they ask for in part covers only the losses they have suffered before you came along, and will only scratch the surface if your business venture fails. If your business succeeds and you are able to pay them back, they are then able to forge another day and begin again.

VC's A DIFFERENT BREED

What VC's Thrive On

VC's thrive on the deal. If they are not making a deal they are not making any money. Once your deal is closed, it will be 2-7 years before they are paid. Therefore, they have to make deals every day to keep deals continuously paying off from the previous 2-7 years. Can you imagine not eating for 2-7 years? Would the quality of your life suffer? How would you maintain respect in your profession? You probably answered no, greatly and could not.

Welcome to the world of VC's.

Why VC's Exist

VC's exist to keep the seeds of humanity planted, cultivated, growing and thriving. Their sole purpose is to ensure the economic flow does not cease. They have a responsibility to humanity that rivals air and water. Without air and water, the world would cease to exist. What I mean is it would turn into a barren planet like Mars/Venus.

Scientists have found compelling evidence that life as we know it, carbon-based, oxygenated and thriving with water and greenery once existed on at least two other planets and potentially many others in our solar system. Therefore, what happened – we can only speculate to the finer details, although at a high level of conjecture we agree that their way of life ceased long before the planet degenerated to the point of not being able to sustain life.

Without VC's

If VC's were not the futurist that they are and did not believe that there is a NEXT BIG worth putting their hard earned dollars into we would not have the basic life apparatus and discoveries we have come to take for granted and cannot live without: pacemakers, cellphones, transportation, running water, electricity, heat etc…imagine if you will.

Data Driven VC's

According to CB Insights, "The venture capital circle of life is: See the Deal, Access the Deal, Win the Deal, and Nurture the Deal. VC'S view data, as a weapon at every step. Venture Capital is a competitive game; smart-data usage gives VCs an unfair advantage. From sourcing deals to analyzing markets faster to finding talent for their portfolio to identifying follow-on investors to pinpointing acquirers, data is power."

Savvy VC's who make use of CB Insights 21-point data driven VC checklist stay far ahead of their competition, and grow the companies they invest in.[1]

CB Insights 21 Point Data Driven VC Checklist

1. Determine who is going to raise before they are raising.
2. See every deal in geographies & industries of interest.
3. Quickly target the best companies.
4. Thought leadership /build your brand.
5. Expand your network.
6. Track your syndicate.
7. Stalk your peer firms.
8. Use lineage tracing to ID companies and investors you should know.
9. Access the quality of investors.
10. Understand rate of follow-on activity.
11. Refine your investment thesis.
12. Analyze health of exit activity in the space.
13. How competitive is the space?
14. What failed?
15. Make them smarter on the industry.
16. Keep them posted on competitors.
17. Collaborate with them on pressing strategic questions.
18. Poach talent for your companies.

19. Pinpoint follow-on investors.
20. Identify potential acquirers.
21. Keep them ahead of the competition.

VC's search for businesses to invest in and they search for investors for joint venture and syndication. Study these 21 data driven points that VCs are utilizing to find business owners and investors, and shore up your business to assure they find you.

What has changed with VC demands?

THE VC LANDSCAPE

Everyone, every industry, every genre is in the VC space. Hardly a day can end without an announcement of millions of dollars being poured into an establishment by a celebrity, a motivational speaker, a singular millionaire or a self-made billionaire. People who yesterday were specialists in their fields and investors are now stepping into the role of Venture Capitalist. With this widening of the landscape, it also changes the climate and the topology. Old standards and guides may fit the top tier of venture funds, but do not preclude the onslaught of entrepreneurs into the market-place.

Women, 20 -30 years old, retirees, founders with limited experience and recent immigrants in all countries are finding themselves on the receiving end of venture capital.

Market share was once reserved for those who had the products, services and more importantly the money to either drive the competition out, or simply capitalize the competition out. Today a VC with $100,000 can provide seed capital to several businesses, who can occupy a segment of the market, provide a 3x or 5x return on the investment and effectively move the VC and themselves to their next level in business.

Founders, clients and consumers are not tied to big business, nor the big box delivery system. They want co-habitation, co-work, co-op markets, live work and play communities. Striving is towards a better future for self, children, mankind and the environment. The success result of life work is no longer the amassing of money, but a life well-spent.

THE VC "EQUITY" POSITION

Majority controlled equity positions "are" no longer the required rule of thumb. VC's on average are taking a 30 – 35% equity stake in companies they are funding, by capitalizing on being diverse investors and not singular owners. They are pursuing use of outside Independent Consultants and Consulting Agencies to monitor, assist in business development, benchmarking and corporate re-organization to achieve ROI.

VC COMPETITION

Globalization has leveled the playing fields across many industries and venture capital is not immune to its affect. Competition is now too great for outlandish demands; founders simply tell VCs with self-serving demands that there are better choices to meet their needs.

FINANCING YOUR NEXT BILLION$$$

CHAPTER 2

WHO IS ON YOUR TEAM?

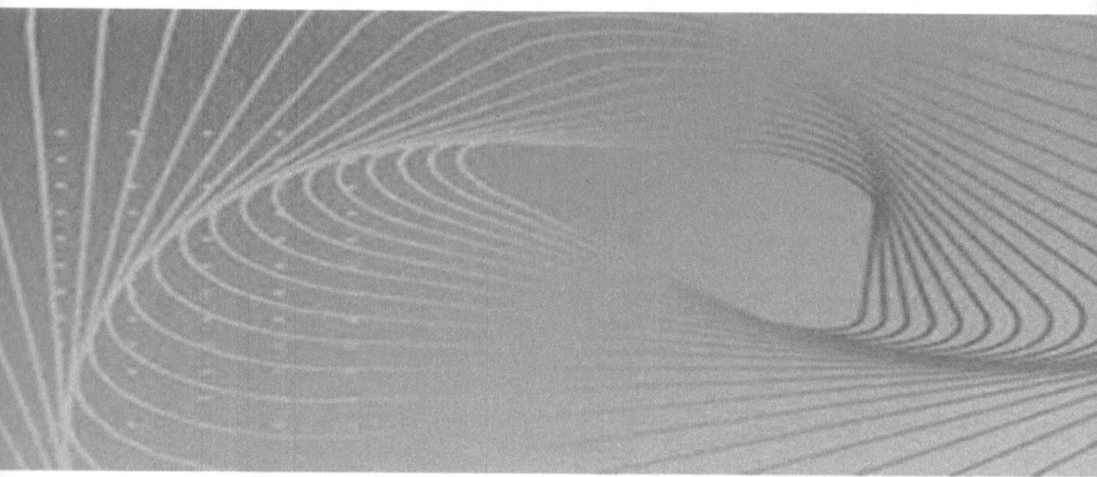

Build a great team

- Finding a co-founder
- Investor expectations around co-founders
- Boards
- Shareholders

Build a great team

WHO IS ON YOUR TEAM

You may think your business is the next Google. That is great. However, your enthusiasm and passion alone does not mean others will buy into it. Venture capital investors will need proof that you are a good investment.

For each of these points you need to show visible proof. A spreadsheet of projected sales is not proof that you can sell. Revenue or commitments to buy are proof. A plan to build and deliver a product is not proof. A working product in the hands of prospects or customers is proof. The more you can actually prove each of these points the more likely you can raise venture capital.

FINDING THE RIGHT CO-FOUNDER

Your best friend, spouse or business co-worker may not be the right co-founder. Either of these may work well as an advisor, and in some instances they work perfectly as a co-founder.

The critical key in your co-founder search is to understand the "offsetting of complementary strengths". Just as with dating you do not want someone who is just like you, nor would you look for someone who is in stark contrast to you. The ideal co-founder is someone whose strengths and attributes complement, compensate and complete your own.

Creating a team with varied experiences and outlooks can give a business a better chance at survival -- perhaps because a co-founder can serve as a built-in editor, mentor, cheerleader and competitor, all in one, forcing the other person to push harder -- if only to not let the other co-founder down.

A great team offers the highest probability of surviving and thriving when it seems that all odds are against the pair.

Investor expectations around co-founders

From the onset of the first meeting with a founder an investor is laser focused on mitigating risk. Many VCs have it written into their standard operating procedures that they will not invest in single-founder companies. While other investors admit too many founders can be difficult and they prefer to work with two or three.

Investors view a single owner company as a potential problem waiting to happen. Who will the founder turn to when major high level issues arise. The company may have the best C-Suite of officers, but they will have a different mindset and priority base that operates apart from ownership. Board members, unless perhaps Working Boards, are not involved in the intricacies of the business.

The big concern is that if a founder gets burned out, or becomes a fatality the succession plan designee may not be able to jump right in and keep things going at the same pace. Without a co-founder often times it is not worth the risk as an investor.

BOARDS

Board members are the fiduciaries who steer the organization towards a sustainable future by adopting sound, ethical, and legal governance and financial management policies, as well as making sure the company has adequate resources to advance its vision. There are three to four boards that you ultimately want to add based on the size and depth of your company.

Board of Directors – The primary board that provides direction and guidance for the vision and mission of the company.

Working Board – The structure of the company may necessitate that each working unit or division have a working board that provides hands-on operational leadership.

Financial Board – Companies large and small are putting financial boards in place for the express purpose of seeking funding and maintaining the financial health of the organization.

Advisory Board – An advisory board can seek out new opportunities and trends that the company needs to be apprised of. These boards also act in the capacity of Mentor.

SHAREHOLDERS

To get a company up and running founders will take on shareholders early on. These relationships, specifically the financial arrangements must be provided to an investor, so that a correct calculation of all obligations will be accounted for, and the investor will know who else has a vested interest in the corporation.

There are two types of shareholders – those who own common shares and individuals with preferred shares. Common shareholders: also known as common stockholders, have voting rights and receive dividends if the company makes a profit and the directors decide not to reinvest all of it.

Shareholders make a financial investment in the corporation, which entitles those with voting shares to elect the directors. Shareholders do not normally have any rights to be involved directly in company management. Their connection to company management is typically via the Board of Directors as described above.

A shareholder, also referred to as a stockholder, is any person, company, or institution that owns at least one share of a company's stock. As equity owners, shareholders are subject to capital gains (or losses) and/or dividend payments as residual claimants on a firm's profits.

When a company generates a profit and accumulates retained earnings, those earnings can be either reinvested in the business or paid out to shareholders as a dividend. Types include: cash, common, preferred, stock, property if the company does well and succeeds.[2]

FINANCING YOUR NEXT BILLION$$$

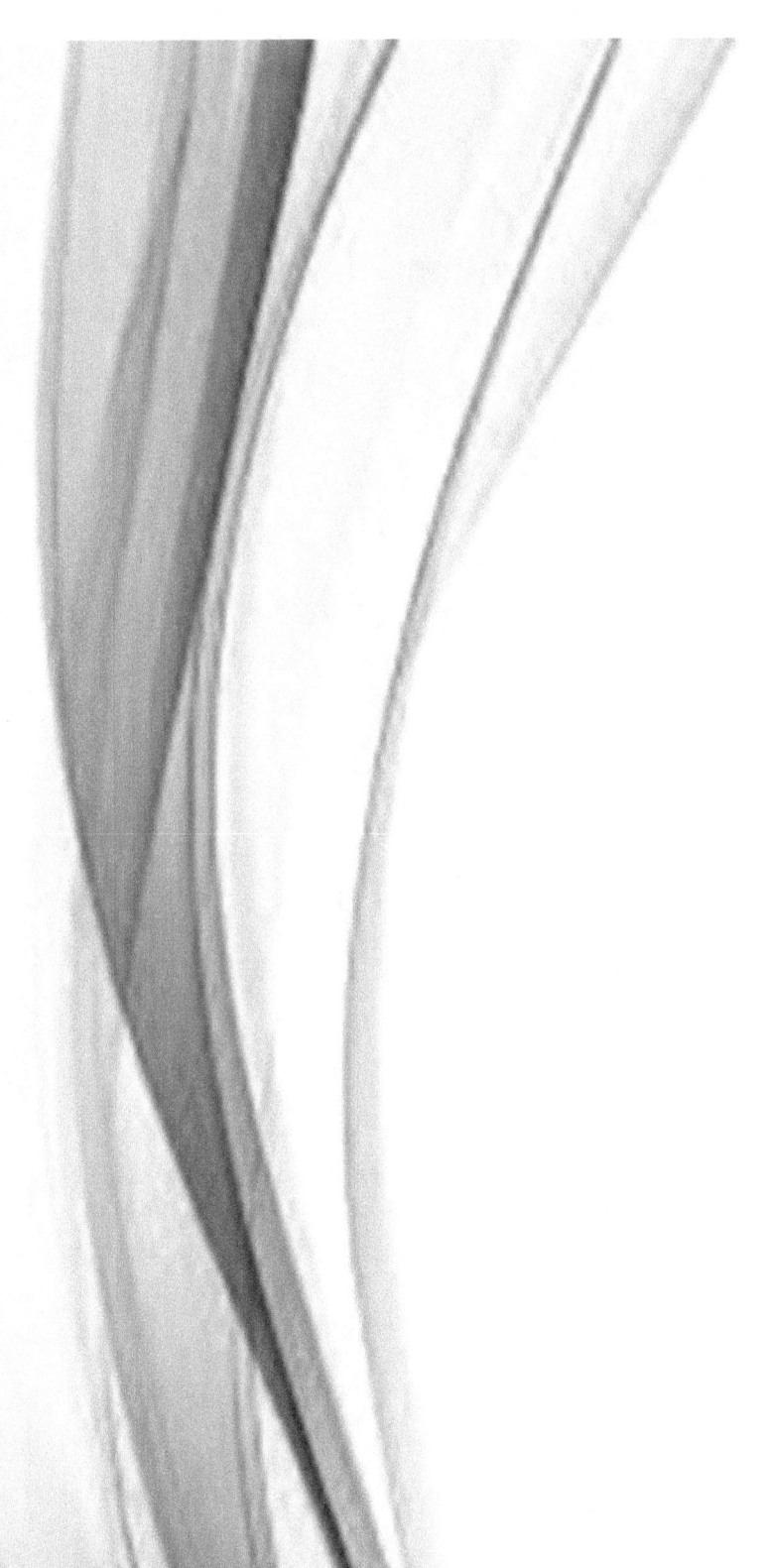

CHAPTER 3

WHICH WAY TO YOUR MARKET

Product development

- Lean Startup methodology
- Product development cycle explained
- Design thinking

Lean startup methodology

Lean startup is a methodology for developing businesses and products that aims to shorten product development cycles and rapidly discover if a proposed business model is viable; this is achieved by adopting a combination of business-hypothesis-driven experimentation, iterative product releases, and validated learning.

The lean startup movement is transforming how new products are built and launched. "Concepts apply both to designing products and to developing a market" The New York Times.

According to the Wall Street Journal "Lean Startup Philosophy helps startups move faster."

PRODUCT DEVELOPMENT CYCLE

No longer are entrepreneurs or business developers sitting in sequestered siloes scratching through volumes of research trying to determine what a customer might want to buy, sell or even think about. In the last 5 years they have turned to a simpler less risky process that quickly designs and validates the minimum viability of a product, using the whole market as a focus test group, and pivoting to a different strategy while still in initial product development.

The lean movement does not have to take over mainstream, in fact it was not designed to do so. The design was to solve an immediate need to bring a product to market. But the millennial and gig economy are forcing the hand of in-experience, low budgets, and no-traction innovators who are attempting to improve their chances of success by following its principles of failing fast and continually re-developing.

DESIGN THINKING

Out with the old, in with the new. The era of static business plans with five year forecasts of complete unknowns is quickly fading. It is being replaced by business models that fit niches, needs and resources.

This distinction is at the heart of the lean start-up approach. It shapes the lean definition of a start-up: a temporary organization designed to search for a repeatable and scalable business model. [2]

YOUR COMPETITION

Understand the external environment

- Assessing the competitive landscape
- Managing political and regulatory risk
- Understanding market risk

Assessing the competitive landscape

Today's savvy entrepreneurs welcome the competition with open source programming, alternative solutions, and "designing towards buyout."

To this end the process of gathering actionable information on a company's competitive intelligence is truly performing supercharged market research.

Competitive intelligence uses many of the same techniques as market research but deploys them to answer highly targeted and specific questions, rather than to gain insight into broad market trends. More people do competitive intelligence than you might think. And it's easy to see why.

In a competitive marketplace, up-to-date information can make the difference between keeping pace, getting ahead, or being left behind. A smart intelligence operation can serve as an early-warning system for disruptive changes in the competitive landscape, whether that change is a rival's new product or pricing strategy or the entrance of an unexpected player into your market. [3]

MANAGE POLITICAL & REGULATORY RISK

Excerpt from World Economic Forum Report Strategic Infrastructure Mitigation of Political & Regulatory Risk in Infrastructure Projects, Prepared in Collaboration with the Boston Consulting Group February 2015. [4]

Political and regulatory risk is one of the major constraints on infrastructure investment decisions. It takes different forms over an infrastructure project's life cycle, from delayed construction permits and community protests to breach of contract, tightened regulations and the non-renewal of licenses. In addition, some broader risks apply throughout the life cycle – changes to taxation laws, for instance, and endemic corruption.

The public sector has to create a stable regulatory environment

The public sector, in particular the national government, can enhance political & regulatory stability by enacting and enforcing appropriate laws and regulation. The specific regulation of each infrastructure sector should be robust, with changes to sector rules that are as predictable as possible. In that regard, it helps to have automatic adaptation mechanisms in place – for example, linking photovoltaic energy feed-in tariffs to the development of module cost, or adapting the duration for a highway concession according to the actual revenue collected from road users. Beyond specific sector regulation, the overall legal architecture must also be considered: it should be conducive to a stable regulatory environment, by providing constitutional guarantees or dedicated investment stability laws.

Legislation alone is not enough, however. The laws and regulation need to be stringently implemented, by the country's executive branch. To mitigate the risk of unexpected and adverse administrative decisions, governments need to ensure a reliable agency set-up, with efficient procurement and permit processes that never compromise on their integrity, as well as strong anti-corruption measures. Investors and the government also need to have confidence in the available dispute-resolution mechanisms, so countries must ensure a judicial capacity that administers the law in an independent, timely and efficient way.

Further protection for investors can be provided by international commitments – hence the ongoing effort to (re-)negotiate bilateral investment treaties (BITs) and investment protection clauses in free trade agreements. Although BITs have been in place for a long time, some countries are still making very little use of them. And many BITs have shortcomings, such as vague protection clauses and controversial arbitration procedures, that cause concern to policy-makers and the public. Those issues are being addressed, however, by emerging new standards and by innovative clauses. So countries might consider increasing their involvement in equitable international commitments as a way of mitigating political & regulatory risk and fostering private investment in infrastructure projects.

The private sector also has means to manage and mitigate political & regulatory risk

Within the framework set by the public sector, the private sector has to find ways of managing and mitigating the political & regulatory risk. For "hard" risks, such as expropriation or currency inconvertibility, companies can make use of financial instruments such as political-risk insurance or guarantees, issued by multilateral organizations, national providers and the private market. In addition, political & regulatory risk could be mitigated by a carefully crafted ownership structure: international co-owners and co-financiers – such as multilateral development banks or institutions from an investor's home country – can have a "deterrence" effect on political intervention, and joint ventures with local partners can enable an infrastructure operator to be viewed as more than just a "foreign investor".

MULTI-STAKEHOLDER ACTION NEEDED

There is no silver bullet for addressing the many facets of political & regulatory risk. The risk-mitigating measures presented in this report all have their uses, and they complement one another. Public and private stakeholders should cooperate, to prioritize areas for action and to create a culture of open dialogue. It will always be a challenge to get the balance right – between the investors' need for regulatory stability and governments' freedom to adjust regulation in line with national priorities. But reasonable stability must be achieved to boost private investment, to increase the quality and quantity of infrastructure projects, and hence to benefit society at large.

UNDERSTANDING MARKET RISK

According to Investopedia "market risk is the possibility of an investor experiencing losses due to factors that affect the overall performance of the financial markets in which he or she is involved. Market risk, also called "systematic risk," cannot be eliminated through diversification, though it can be hedged against in other ways."5

Investors are starkly aware of the risks of investment, and take pre-cautionary steps such as deep dive due diligence which we will discuss in detail in section 5, chapter 10. It is important to understand the risks associated with your product and service offerings, this will make it more palatable to understand the investor's perspective and perception.

The three primary risks that you need to be aware of when seeking venture capital are 1. Management Risk, 2. Credit Risk and 3. Market Risk.

1. Management Risk – Your team, your board, your corporate governance has direct effect and can impede bottom-line outcomes to your financial capabilities. Step outside of your comfort zone and select people who are beyond your sphere of friends and colleagues. Expertise in industry and responsibilities is what you need.
2. Credit Risk – Investors are concerned that you may default or will not be unable to pay back their investment as agreed. You will need to set-up mechanisms such as insurance policies, savings accounts, and contingency lines of credit to mitigate credit risk. SanPete Financial Group, a venture capital firm headquartered in Atlanta, Georgia USA instructs each of its clients to negotiate upfront a convertible note option; thereby inserting a contingency for investment repayment. At the end of the investment period if the business is unable to pay the initial investment plus interest as agreed the total outstanding amount converts to a commercial business loan note with an already agreed upon rate and term.
3. Market Risk – Market risk or systematic risk refers to the overall economy and can bring down the value of an individual investment in a company regardless of that company's growth, revenues, earnings, management, and capital structure. This type of risk is out of your or the investors control to halt, but you must be aware of market conditions and impacts in your industry. Discuss these impacts candidly and provide your contingency plans in the event market risks surface.

YOUR VALUE PROMISE

Know the target market

- Get to know your customer
- Define your target market in 6 steps

Get to know your customer

With Big Data analytics available at a single touch, it is impossible not to gather hordes of information on your target market. But what does that really tell you about the customer who will actually call you, knock on your door or respond to your marketing? Not so much.

There is always that chasm between what a person says or responds to in a survey versus what they do in a singular setting, based on a given set of variables. My good friend and colleague Huda Gregg, CEO of E-Choice Insurance Services says "I feel there is nothing like a good old fashioned meeting."

It is an imperative in a technology driven world to connect on a deeper level with customers.

Creating quality products is an essential part of building a business that thrives. But it isn't the only part of the equation.

Take the time to figure out how to transcend the transaction and create an emotional bond with your customers. It is possible even if your business operates entirely online.

It takes more consistent effort, but the rewards that come from creating loyal customers are more than worth it.

Getting to "Yes" in a venture capital raise is 100% relationship. It is the belief in the founder's ability to stay the course through the ups and downs in bringing a new product or service to the marketplace. It is the gut feeling that investors feel about your teams and their loyalty to the brand and the process they must traverse to go from idea to market share leader. The relationship bond that you forge with the venture capitalist will give them the confidence to say "Yes, I will invest in you."

6 STEPS TO TARGET MARKET

1. What problem do you solve? – Dig deep beyond what you have stated in your brochures or marketing materials and really get to the heart of the

problems that you actually solve or the problems that you could be better at solving.

2. Who do you currently serve? – Why are they buying from you, or why would they buy from you. Answer these questions and you will know how to add customers.

3. Exactly what does your competition do? – All too often businesses try hard to offer a better widget. Could the competition be missing a selling opportunity? What niche are they not serving? Might you partner with them if you offered a complimentary service?

4. Which specific demographics do you want to target – Tesla an electric car brand markets to a specific demographic client who is in the market for an electric vehicle. While Chevrolet, Nissan and several other automakers also sell an electric vehicle their customers are in a totally different target market, notwithstanding price point alone.

5. Define the Psychographics of your market – Psychographics is the classification of people according to their attitudes or aspirations. These are the more personal characteristics like attitudes, values, hobbies, and behavior and they have a huge impact on identifying your target market. How is your product or service going to fit into your target market's lifestyle? What are the most appealing features to your target? Where does your target audience go for information? These are some of the questions you can answer once you identify the psychographics of your target customer.6

6. Put it all in perspective – Is my pricing both affordable and profitable? Does my target audience have expendable resources to afford my prices? Why will my target audience buy? How does my product/service benefit my target audience? What value does my product/services add? Does my messaging speak to my target audience?

FINANCING YOUR NEXT BILLION$$$

CHAPTER 4

SCALABILITY, AGILITY, ADAPTABILITY

Growth

- Capitalization
- Scalability
- Agility
- Adaptability

The company has the ability to invest the new funds properly and scale operations rapidly.

CAPITALIZATION

When seeking capital partners every aspect of the business has to be accounted for. Current financial relationships, debt exposure, stocks issued, ownership percentages all are factored into the valuation of the business. Utilize a capitalization table to visually demonstrate companies position with outstanding obligations and its resulting post-money valuation after equity infusion.

CAPITALIZATION TABLE

"A cap table is a spreadsheet for a startup company or early-stage venture that lists all the company's securities such as common shares, preferred shares, warrants, who owns them, and the prices paid by the investors for these securities. It indicates each investor's percentage of ownership in the company, the value of their securities and dilution over time. Cap tables are created first before other company documents in the early stages of a startup or venture. After a few rounds of financing, the cap tables become complex and it lists the potential sources of funding, initial public offerings, mergers and acquisitions and other transactions."

In addition to recording transactions, a cap table also comprises many legal documents such as stock issuances, transfers, cancellations, conversion of debt to equity, and other documents. The executives must manage all these transactions and documents accurately to show the events since the company's inception. The simplest form of cap tables lists the shareholders at the beginning and their respective share ownership. Venture capitalists, entrepreneurs and investment analysts to analyze important events such as ownership dilution, employee stock options and issue of new securities use cab tables.

SIMPLIFY THE CAP TABLE

Simplify your cap table to yield the maximum benefit. You can find numerous spreadsheet templates that allows for the addition of information and figures related to your business. The first row should indicate the total number of shares of the company. The subsequent rows should list the following:

- Authorized shares: Number of shares the company is allowed to issue.
- Outstanding shares: Number of shares held by all shareholders in the company.
- Unissued Shares: Number of shares that have not been issued.
- Shares reserved for stock option plan: Unissued shares reserved for future hires. A separate table in the capitalization table should include the following:
- Names of shareholders: The names of shareholders who have bought shares in the company.
- Shares owned by each shareholder: The number of shares held by each shareholder.
- Stock options: Stock options owned by each shareholder.
- Fully diluted shares: Total number of outstanding shares (helps shareholders determine the value of their shares).
- Options remaining: Number of remaining shares available to be optioned.

The company's founders are listed first in the table, followed by executives and other employees who own equity and then investors such as angel investors and venture capitalists.

FINANCING YOUR NEXT BILLION$$$

CHAPTER 5

LEGAL BASICS

LEGAL BASICS

The company must be structured to take on venture capital funding, prior to beginning venture capital funding rounds.

Legal basics

- Register your business entity to attract venture capital
- Intellectual Property
- VC Financing documents

REGISTER YOUR BUSINESS TO ATTACT VENTURE CAPITAL

It is well worth noting and understanding a very important fact about VC's. That fact is they have investors. Most VC's are organized as partnerships which means the income it receives passes through to its partners (investors). Many VC's have tax-exempt investors such as pension funds and foundations, and the income you would pass through to them could be taxed as unrelated business taxable income. A corporation avoids this issue. (VC's also have to keep their investors satisfied)

It's wise to set yourself up as a C-Corp from the outset, or switch to a C-Corp before you begin your venture capital raise. Most venture capitalists are unwilling—or unable—to invest in any other business entity.

I am sure the burning question in your mind is 'why a C-Corp?"

The first reason is that C corporations make it very easy to transfer stock (ownership) and are able to have multiple classes of stock such as preferred stock, which gives the holder certain preferences over common stockholders (VC's always get preferred stock)

The second reason is LLCs or Limited Liability Corporations present tax implications, which deter—and in some cases even prevent—venture capitalists from investing. LLCs are especially problematic because venture capitalists have a strong focus on liquidity events. To convert an equity investment into profits for VCs, startups typically need to IPO or be bought be another company. The problem is, it's rather complicated—and sometimes even impossible—to transfer or sell partial ownership in an LLC.

The third reason why VCs prefer C-Corps over S-Corps is simply that all corporations are not created equally. Here's why:

1. S-Corps present the same tax problems for VCs as LLCs do.

Like LLCs, S-Corps are "pass-through" entities, meaning that the S-corp doesn't pay federal income tax. Rather, the S-Corp's shareholders pay federal income tax on the company's taxable income, based on their pro-rated stock ownership. VCs simply don't want to deal with this sort of complexity.[1]

2. Most VC firms can't legally be shareholders in an S-Corp.

To legally invest in an S-Corp, shareholders must be U.S. citizens or residents and "natural persons." Not only does this rule out foreign investors, it also rules out most domestic VC money, which typically comes from VC firms that are set up as partnerships or LLCs. In other words, they are not "natural persons."

Also, VC firms with tax-exempt partners legally can't invest in S-Corps because they're pass-through entities.[1]

3. Only C-Corps can offer preferred stock.

Even if you could find American-based individual venture capitalists who legally could invest in your company, they would likely avoid your S-Corp. Here's why: S-Corps can only offer common stock, not preferred stock. And preferred stock—which pays higher dividends and puts stockholders first in line to get paid out in a liquidity event—is exactly what VCs expect when they take a significant risk on your company.1

4. C-Corps don't have limitations on growth.

Unlike a C-Corp, an S-Corp is limited to only 100 shareholders. Although this may sound like a lot for a startup that has yet to issue a single stock, this upper limit can be reached rather quickly, especially if a cash-strapped startup offers extra perks in the form of employee stock. VCs are likely to worry about a startup's inability to grow once the 100 shareholder threshold has been reached. What if you've maxed out on shareholders and still need to raise more money to truly scale your company?1

INTELLECTUAL PROPERTY

According to the World Intellectual Property Organization (WIPO) Intellectual property is an integral part of value creation in a technology-based enterprise.2 Value creation is a critical element in obtaining venture capital for businesses. The appropriate use of the intellectual property system is a powerful tool for competition, stability and mitigation of risks on capital investments.

The Importance of Intellectual Property Asset Management

Exclusive rights

Founders must show substantiated proof that they own exclusive rights to their intellectual property and its' associated systems. The IP will often be the main assets from which a business technology-based enterprise benefits. The appropriate use of the intellectual property system may contribute to bring high rates of return on capital, which is crucial in order to attract venture capital investors.

ECONOMIC VALUE

The economic value of a patent, a trademark, software, a domain name, and any intellectual property must be carefully weighed in the analysis of which companies deserve to receive venture capital investments. Not all intangible assets are equal. The venture capitalist will utilize various techniques for evaluating the intangible assets of the target enterprise and make decisions on when and whether to invest based on such valuation.

Security of intellectual property

Securing IP is of vital importance, and business owners need to factor in the on-going costs associated with patents and their protection.

While there are several IP security issues that raise concern for venture capitalist there are two glaring items that cross all industries and sectors; that of software and employees who may claim to own the IP.

"Viral" Free Software a Worry for Tech Investors

Funding software and tech start-ups also raises IP concerns, said Katherine Gardner of Gunderson Dettmer Stough Villeneuve Franklin & Hachigian LLP (New York), who represents tech companies and venture firms.3

One issue is the selling company's use of open source software, Gardner said. Open source is provided under a license under the Open Source Initiative which requires redistribution without payment and allows users to modify and create derivatives, she said. Some open source licenses, such as the GNU General Public License, are considered "viral" or "copyleft," meaning that licensees who use the code must license their entire work to anyone who comes into possession of a copy. This worries VCs, Gardner said. Among other things, they will want to know how a company tracks its use of open source and whether it has policies in place to prevent misuse.3

I helped design and develop the IP

Employment-related issues are another key concern, Gardner said.3

It is an imperative that non-compete documentation be created by a legal firm who understands IP and it's many nuances. Businesses should have a system in place where they review the non-compete agreement and require a signature at the entering and exiting of all employees of the company.

VC Financing documents

Annually, the venture industry closes several thousand financing rounds, each consuming considerable time and effort on the part of investors, management teams and attorneys. Conservatively, the industry spends some $200 million in direct legal fees annually to close private financing rounds. In other words, the venture industry goes through an expensive and inefficient process of "re-inventing the flat tire" on a daily basis. By providing an industry-embraced set of model documents that can be used in venture capital financings the time and cost of financings are greatly reduced and therefore principals time is freed from reviewing hundreds of pages of unfamiliar documents, thereby allowing parties to focus on high-level issues trade-offs of the deal at hand.[4]

The National Venture Capital Association's model VC Financing documents are listed is below. You can download, review and familiarize yourself with the documents that you will be signing at the close of your venture capital raise: http://bit.ly/ModelVCDocs. The investor will provide you with their respective proprietary documents.

- Voting Agreement
- Term Sheet
- Stock Purchase Agreement
- Right of First Refusal and Co-Sale Agreement
- Model Legal Opinion
- Management Rights Letter
- Investor Rights Agreement
- Indemnification Agreement
- Certificate of Incorporation
- LPA Insert Language on CFIUS
- Life Science Confidential Disclosure Agreement
- Sample H.R. Best Practices for Addressing Harassment & Discrimination
- Sample Code of Conduct Policy
- Sample H.R. Policies for Addressing Harassment & Discrimination
- Sample H.R. Policies for Attracting & Retaining Diverse Talent
- Sample Diversity & Inclusion Policies — SF Family Friendly Workplace Policy
- Sample Diversity Policies — NY Paid Family Leave Policy
- Sample Diversity & Inclusion Policies — San Francisco Paid Parental Leave Policy

FINANCING YOUR NEXT BILLION$$$

FINANCING YOUR NEXT BILLION$$$

CHAPTER 6

KNOW YOUR INVESTOR

- Into the mind of the equity investor
- Debt versus equity
- Types of capital providers

INTO THE MIND OF THE EQUITY INVESTOR

When your plan is to approach a venture capitalist for equity funding keep in mind the VC's two primary layers that were talked about in the Introduction. Layer one – The accumulation of funds for equity and debt funding, and Layer two – The types of product/services that are of interest. Where does a VC want to invest their money and where do they want to spend their time? These are of extreme importance to your success in getting funded because they go directly to the heart of the VC, and become their "WHY do I want to fund this project.

VC's ask themselves 'why' every day. In fact, before I get out of bed every morning, I ask myself Why. Why did I wake up this morning, why am I here, why am I going to do something today? All these and many more questions come from VC'S daily. Your challenge is to determine how to insert your project/service into their WHY. A VC's why determines what will get funded, when and to whom.

How to do it? How do you go from your wants, needs and why to putting the VC's why in the forefront? This should be as easy as taking candy from a baby, but as we all know, that never turns out the way you think it will. The baby seems to hang onto the candy with a strength that the best wrestler cannot match.

Let me give you some tips to guide you. First, and foremost, you will find it far simpler to change your mind set by engrafting the following skills, and learning to wield the five strategies that you'll find below. As you read the list and the strategies, ask yourself the following question. How many of these skills am I employing and how can I adapt these strategies to my business today, right now?

There are 5 key strategies billionaires have used to build their wealth, which by the way is the money you are asking them to allow you to use.

1. BILLIONAIRES create products with an abundance of value.
2. BILLIONAIRES insert themselves as a service provider in a high-growth industry.
3. BILLIONAIRES improve systems of communication.
4. BILLIONAIRES create consumable products.
5. BILLIONAIRES invest in real estate.

To execute these 5 strategies, you will need to do the following actions every day, from now on. The below 10 directives, must become your mantra and you must make measurable action on each of them every day in a small or big way.

To make sure that I adhere to this list I write down each one every day in my journal, and I write what I did that day for each of the ten items. Is it easy? No! Is it worth it? Yes!

1. Leverage an abundance mentality and laser-focus your mindset
2. Become an expert at business networking
3. Overcome the often-stifling fear of failure
4. Effectively manage your time
5. Create long-term goals and take daily action towards them
6. Never give up no matter how tough things might be
7. Focus the power of your thoughts on the positive over the negative
8. Never look for shortcuts or try to cut corners
9. Understand the underlying principles of sales and marketing
10. Become a fervent brand-builder

FINANCING YOUR NEXT BILLION$$$

FINANCING YOUR NEXT BILLION$$$

CHAPTER 7

THE RIGHT PITCH

- De-risking your startup
- How to prepare investor pitch deck
- Questions to expect from investors
- Tips on presenting in public

DERISKING YOUR STARTUP

Consultants monitor on behalf of investor
- Up to 1000 companies invested in
- ROI: 3-5x investment

HOW TO PREPARE AN INVESTOR PITCH DECK

Now that venture capital has become a household word with the onslaught of accelerator incubators and private investors expending from $100 to millions as commonplace as Starbucks, finding a pitch deck template is just a google search away. But is the template or the many directional tips you get on a google search the right pitch deck for you?

Your pitch deck has to be just that, your pitch deck. It has to speak with your voice to authentically tell your story, present your vision so ultimately you are positioned to own the outcome of the venture. The venture capitalist is only there to assist you along the journey.

A pitch deck is usually a 10-20 slide presentation designed to give a short summary of your company, your business plan and your startup vision. I recommend that you prepare a 20 slide master presentation that includes all the necessary detail about your venture. We will discuss later how you will utilize your master presentation to create subsets that will meet the needs of where and to whom you will be presenting.

Opportunities to present to an investor or an investor's representative can arise at any moment, you and your presentation must be ready. Your presentation should be capable of presenting deftly thru 5 major mediums. It must be mobile ready, email ready, multi-exchange platform ready, stage ready and most of all you must be ready to present the pitch without a deck, when the opportunity arises.

THE PITCH DECK

For the DIY Entrepreneur there are several online sharing tools that range from free to $59 a month for all the best features. Just don't get bogged down or lost in the presentation and fail to get your point across. Here are 7 of the top presentations software platforms that can be utilized across the 5 major mediums.

1. Prezi was ranked in 2018 by PC World ranked as the most innovative of presentation software companies. Great for those who serious about storytelling.1
2. Google Slides offers a simplified web-based PowerPoint style tool which can be used to quickly make and share decks. This solution offers a great tool for collaborating with co-founders and advisors, as well as easier sharing via email or directly online.
3. SalesHandy is one of the solutions floated on Quora for those who want to see what's happening after they hit send on their deck. If you're the type of entrepreneur who is going to be laying awake at night watching your inbox to see if you get any responses or you're a data geek who wants every metric possible to keep honing and improving your deck, then check it out.1
4. DocSend is another presentation tool which gives startups detailed data on deck viewers like SaleHandy. DocSend also provides an online viewer so

you never have to worry about downloads, as well as online voice meeting and screen share tools for presenting virtually.
5. Slidebean has become of the best known alternatives to PowerPoint among the new startup crowd. It does offer some great looking out of the box templates, and seems to be in tune with the startup ecosystem.

THE PRESENTATION

Email

On the other hand, a pitch presentation that you're planning to email should be completely self-explanatory. It's going to be seen on a laptop monitor, so small font is not so bad.

Mobile

All mobile devices are not equal. Look at the presentation on Apple, Android and all tablet sizes. This can easily be done at an Apple or Microsoft store. Just ask to see a demo of each device.

Demo Day

A demo day presentation, should be very visual and contain very little text. It's going to be seen from afar and you're going to do all the talking.

Your Stage Presence

Rehearse, rehearse, rehearse

1st 5 minutes – Convey what you propose is worth their time to LISTEN!

2nd 5 minutes – What's unique. Why you, Who will buy? Can or have you proven the model? Got traction? Who do you compete with?

3rd 5 minutes – Ask for what you NEED…How will you spend it…How much ROI? When can I expect ROI?

Last 5 minutes – What questions do you have for me?

AIRBNB PITCH DECK - THE DECK THEY USED TO RAISE THEIR FIRST $600K

- Problem.

- Solution.
- Market Validation.
- Market Size.
- Product.
- Business Model.
- Marketing Plan.
- Competition.
- Founding Board
- Fundraising

FINANCING YOUR NEXT BILLION$$$

FINANCING YOUR NEXT BILLION$$$

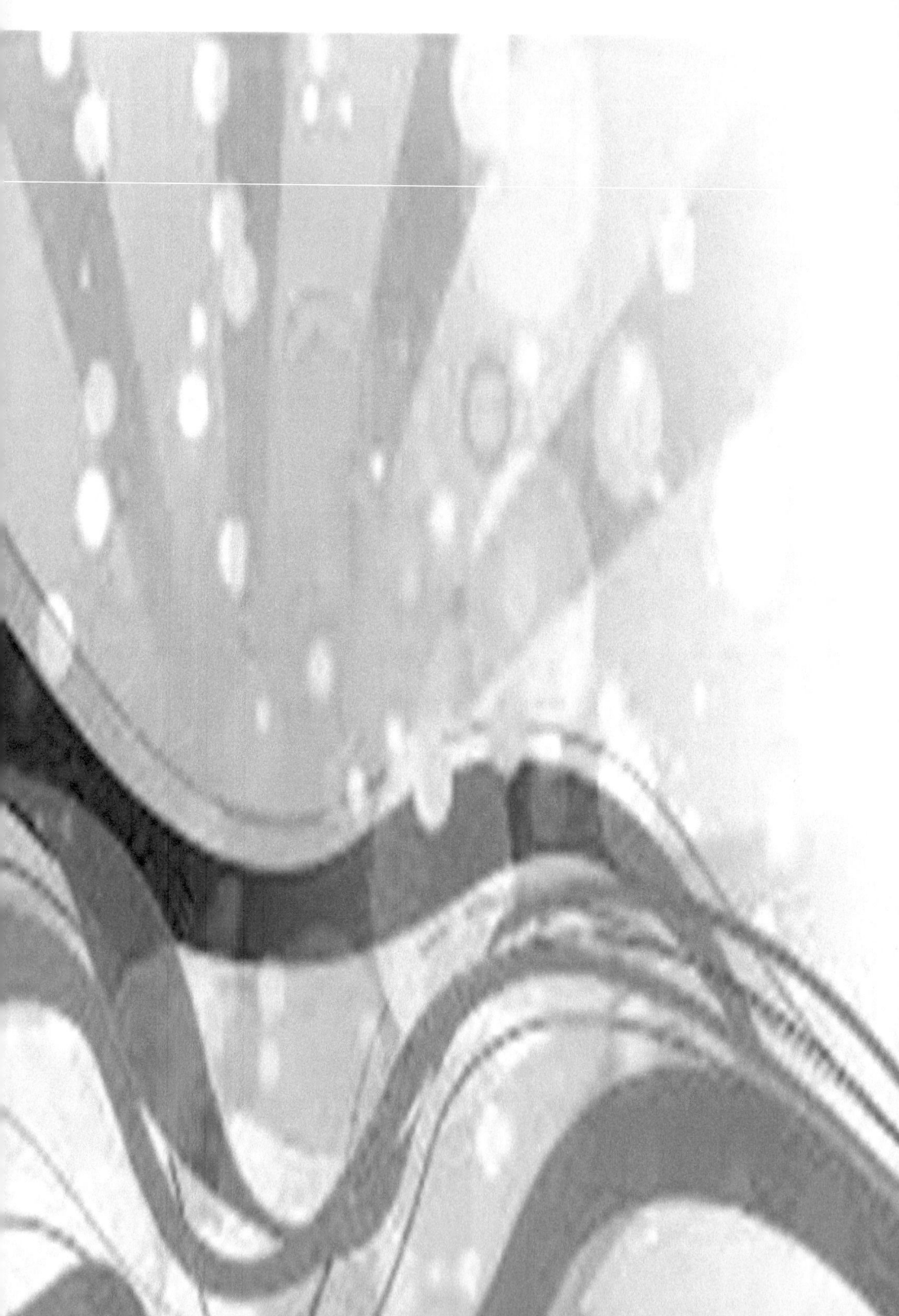

CHAPTER 8

HOW DEEP IS DUE DILIGENCE

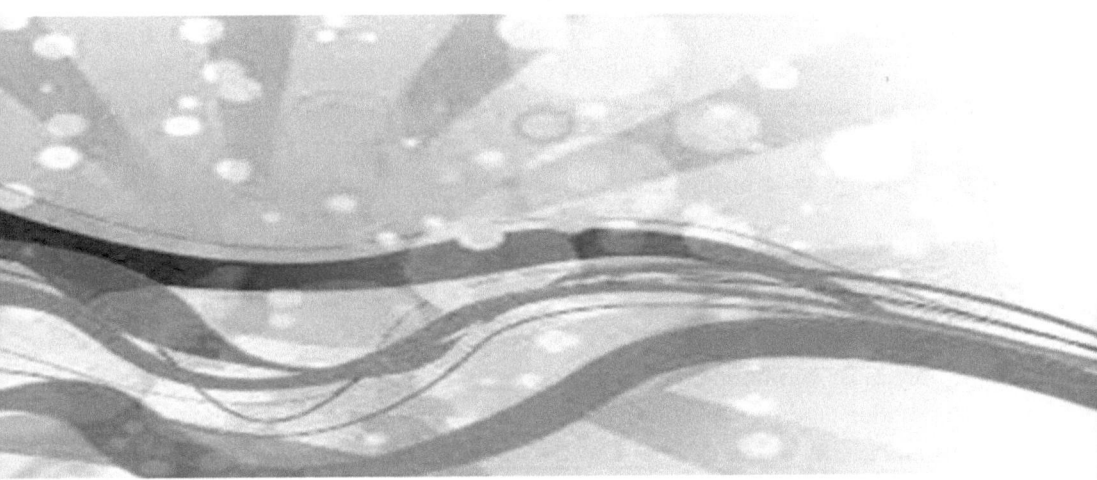

What level of due diligence should I expect?

Market and Competition

Supporting data for your market size

Detailed analysis of competitors

WHAT LEVEL OF DUE DILIGENCE SHOULD I EXPECT?

John Vyge, in his book The Dragons' Den Guide to Investor-Ready Business Plans tells us that:

"The level of due diligence performed by an investor depends on the investors financial and emotional tolerance risk. One investor may request reams of information while another might write a check without reading your business plan. If you are lucky enough to be considering investment capital from two different investors, the treatment from each during the due diligence process may determine whom you eventually get into bed with. On the one hand, detail oriented, hard-nosed investors, who ask you a million questions can be annoying, but may be just the investor type you need. They may have the financial analytical skill to bring your business to the next financial milestone, or point you in the right direction. One the other hand cordial investors who ask for very little follow-up may be viewed as lax, but may be savvy enough to know a good deal when they see it, and would be just the type to leave you alone to build the business."[4]

To achieve a successful funding, you will need to go through due diligence. Those that get through it without a scratch are the businesses who see it as a way to improve their business. They see beyond the variety of investor personality types with focused attention on what each investor brings to the table both financially and strategically. Keep in mind that due diligence is not merely gathering information from you, it is about you, and how your business operates.

Due diligence is both a learning and growing process.

MARKET AND COMPETITION

Not only must you understand the product and services that you are providing you must understand the consumers that will purchase your products today, tomorrow and in the future. It is not enough to offer a competitive rate, competitive price or a competitive product. Your marketing needs to support the changing values, trends, financial and migration patterns of the market place.

Amazon's massive boxed delivery system is a trend that has re-introduced the catalogue shopper of the 50's with several new twists. No longer are items shipped from a warehouse in a central location in the country, rather large storage facilities have popped up strategically throughout the country harnessing data on the buying habits from region, to a zip code assuring products are on hand for next day delivery.

SUPPORTING DATA FOR YOUR MARKET SIZE

For every data metric, that you show you must be able to provide supporting documentation that there exists a market ready to consume your product or services. As you identify potential customers in your target market, segment them with precise granularity, this will give you the opportunity to demonstrate the "why" a customer will purchase your product over another product of similar value and cost.

Economic conditions have a great impact on purchase decisions because it is the single most changing factor in supply and demand. The cost of goods sold the ability to move products to the customer, safety & health, job market and potential; are all areas that need to illustrate so that is shows a clear picture of how your product and services address each of these conditions.

DETAILED ANALYSIS OF COMPETITORS

How viable is your business idea versus that of your competitors who are in the market, and who are entering the market? To make your product better, more value, or more appealing it is important to know what your competition is providing. To whom are services provided, and how do they deliver them? Are their customers satisfied with the service level they are receiving? Are they a sole source provider of a particular service, brand, or product? Knowing and articulating the answers to these questions will carve you a design path to serve your target market, and will provide opportunity to serve the gaps that your competitors leave open.

FINANCING YOUR NEXT BILLION$$$

FINANCING YOUR NEXT BILLION$$$

CHAPTER 9

DUE DILIGENCE REQUIRED INFORMATION

H1 Required Due Diligence Information

ONLINE APPLICATION

You will be required to complete an online application. Handwritten or email attachment information will not be accepted. Be certain to answer each question completely; all questions must be answered in detail. You are able to cut and paste as necessary but do not answer any question with a reference to the business planning documentation or website. Funding dollar values must be expressed in the dollar value of the country that your venture capital investor will be appropriating funds from.

SECTION ONE

1. Name of Project:

2. Contact information for the Corporation or Ownership Group:

(a) Name of Principal:
(b) Company Name:
(c) Address:
(d) City:State: Zip Code: Country:
(e) Telephone:
(f) Cell phone:
(g) Skype address:
(h) Email:
(i) Company EIN (if applicable):

3. Contact information of Registered Agent for the Corporation or Ownership Group:

(a) Name:
(b) Address:
(c) City: State: Country:
(d) Telephone:
(e) Fax:
(f) Email:

4. Patriot Act information: (please provide a copy of your passport or driver's license)

(a) Citizen of (state the country):
(b) Passport number:
(c) Place and date passport issued:
(d) Expiration date of passport:

5. The Applicant is:

(a) Corporation or Ownership Group:
(b) Individual:

6. Funding Amount (US Dollars): What is the amount of the funding request, that is, the amount of funds (including working capital) that the Applicant is seeking for the Project for all phases and what % of the total project costs does this represent:

Amount in USD: $

% of Project total cost: %

7. Your investment in the Project:

1) Have already contributed: $ USD and/or
2) Plan to contribute: $ USD

8. USE OF PROCEEDS -The advanced sum will be used to: (Explain)

9. Describe Your Asset/Project in a brief Executive Summary (do not refer to other

documents, cut and paste, if necessary):

10. Do you propose to develop and hold the Asset/Project as an investment or is it proposed to develop for sale upon completion? (Explain length to complete Project and exit strategies.)

11. Do you hold all necessary approvals in order to immediately proceed with the proposed development/project? (Explain)

12. At what address is the Asset/Project located?

13. Nearest airport information:

(a)   Name:
(b)   Airport Code:
(c)   Driving time from airport to the location of the Asset/Project:
(d)   Name of the nearest major city:

14. Financial information for Asset/Project

(a)   If you already own the Asset/Project, do you require the Funder to refinance any existing debt? (Please explain and indicate amount):
(b)   If you wish to acquire the Asset/Project, what will be the sale/acquisition price?
(c)   For how many years do you require the Funder's Advance?
(d)   What is the present equity interest in the Asset/Project [i.e. how much of the Principal(s)' money has been invested in the Project]?
(e)   How much is required to complete full development, including full equipment and full furnishings?
(f)   How will the interest and principal be repaid (amortization)?
(g)   Is the interest to be paid from day one or capitalized (if so, for what period)?
(h)   Are you offering corporate guarantees, bank or similar guarantees? Government or similar guarantees?
(i)   What form of collateral are you offering on Asset/Project? (Land, patents, contracts, etc.)

15. Provide a short outline of the management team's past experience in the field covered by the subject Project. (Please list professional advisors in this Section, i.e. CPA/Attorneys):

16. Provide information regarding what collateral, if any, you offer:

17. Name the Funders who are considering or have considered your Application and advise the result:

18. If you are applying to us via an Intermediary, please confirm the extent of the

Intermediary fee agreement, expressed as a percentage of the Advance sum:

SECTION TWO

ALL applicants must provide this information – if the project is a start-up, please provide projections.

Please insert Financial Models, Balance Sheets etc. below showing data for a minimum period of five years. Examples of typical questions are outlined below.

1. Provide quarterly gross income for five years, including operating income, rents, sales, cash injection, before interest and principal payments.

2. Provide quarterly operating expenses for five years, excluding interest and principal payments and development costs.

3. Show end of years 1, 2, 3, 4, 5 balance, deducting total year's operating expenses from the total year's gross income.

4. Show, quarter by quarter, the sums you require to be advanced for development purposes.

5. Show end of years 1, 2, 3, 4, 5 projected value of the Asset/Project

6. Timetable envisaged for project preparation through to completion.

7. Repayment plan.

8. Exit Strategy.

FINANCING YOUR NEXT BILLION$$$

FINANCING YOUR NEXT BILLION$$$

CHAPTER 10

60 MINUTES WITH AN INVESTOR

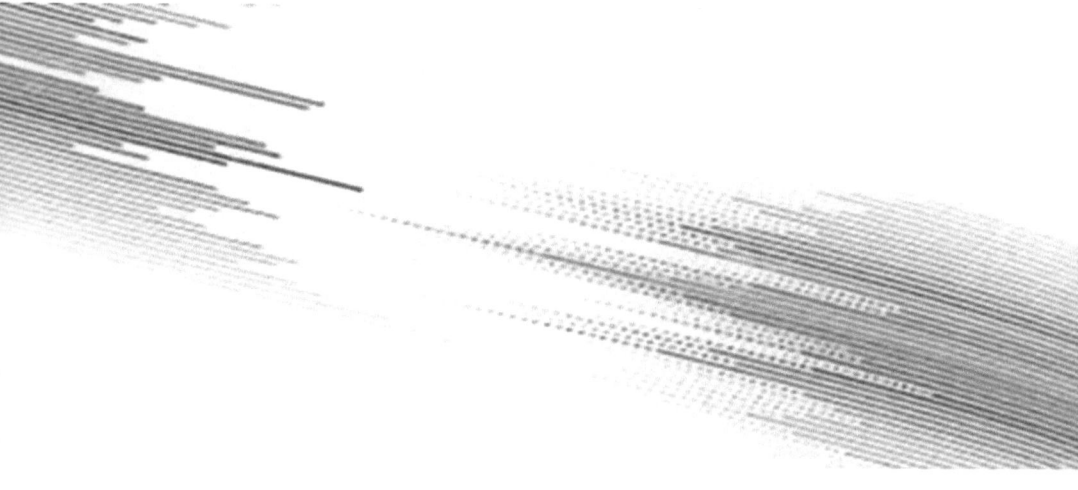

60 Minutes with an Investor

Open with 3 slides

Presenting a full story

10 Steps to Assure a Successful Capital Raise

60-MINUTES WITH AN INVESTOR

When you get a 60-minute appointment with an investor do not assume that you get 60-minutes' worth of attention. You don't. In fact, the typical attention span in an hour-long meeting goes something like this what you will learn from this video.

Use the first 5 minutes to earn the investor's attention for the next 15 minutes, which in turn will interest the investor enough to listen for another 30 minutes. In those 5 minutes, you need to convey the main reasons why an investor should love your business, and invest in you.

OPEN WITH 3 SLIDES

1. What will change? Explain what is the discontinuous shift, break-through, or innovation that opens the window to create a substantial new company.
2. What you do: A one-sentence explanation of what your company provides to capitalize on that big change. It still surprises me how often we can get 20 minutes into a meeting without a clear picture of exactly what a company does.
3. Fast facts: Lay out the key metrics for your business: when were you founded? How many employees? What stage of development / market traction? What are you looking to raise? This helps the investor put the rest of the presentation in context.

At this point, the first 5 minutes are almost up and that leaves 15 minutes to run through an agenda slide, which covers all the usual ground (e.g., product, market size, team, etc.). Pause 30 seconds and check in with your listeners. Most likely, they have seen businesses in the past which they think are similar. Maybe they have some biases based on prior experience in a similar market. If it is a first time presentation more than likely they will just ask you to keep going, not so on the second and third presentation. Prepare, prepare, prepare.

PRESENT A FULL STORY

There are many ways to present the full story of the business here are some pitfalls to avoid in each area:

- Pain: Be very clear about the problem you are solving. For consumer concepts, talk about user needs; for enterprise ideas, show a detailed understanding of your customer's pain. If you cannot convince an investor there's something broke or missing, they will not be interested in a solution.
- Solution: It's not possible every time (e.g. for infrastructure software), but whenever you can, a demo is worth a thousand words. Failing that, use screen shots and the work-flow charts to bring the solution alive.
- Market size: If it's a new market, explain how many users or customers there are for the product/ service, how this number grows over time, and how much each of these users/customers is worth. If it's a replacement market, explain how big the existing market is today and how much you expect your solution to shrink it, through lower prices. One thing not to do is to put up huge numbers from some market study without any details behind them.
- Competition: Identify all the competitors, so that investors don't discover them afterwards. Pro- actively explain how you are different.

- Team: If the investor is interested, they will want to know about the team, so it's worth spending a couple of minutes on the founders' backgrounds, highlighting any special talents or experiences that make them well-suited to building the business.
- Financials: Don't get lost in your numbers. Keep it simple, show on a timeline how you would spend the money (e.g., headcount) to achieve specific milestones (e.g., launching the service).
  - Plan and prepare **to get through the entire presentation in 20 minutes, so that there is lots of time for discussion afterwards.**

10 STEPS TO ASSURE A SUCCESSFUL CAPITAL RAISE

1) Identify your current financial stage.
2) Determine best structure for your company to attract investors.
3) Develop Investor Business Plan and Investor Pitch.
4) Target and engage the right investors for your stage.
5) Prepare for warm introductions to Investors.
6) Prepare to attend the right meetings including accelerator and VC events.
7) Prepare to get on stage.
8) Reorganize your teams to include members and boards that bring value.
9) Receive feedback to attain continuous improvement.
10) Achieve Funding.

FINANCING YOUR NEXT BILLION$$$

CHAPTER 11
BREAKING DOWN BARRIERS TO PROJECT FUNDING

6 Things Billionaires do Differently

How MONEY is Made

What is your Relationship with Money?

The Strength of Money

6 THINGS BILLIONAIRES DO DIFFERENTLY

When billionaires invest in or buy as much as 15% ... 10% ... even 5% of a company's stock, their mindset is they are in the driver's seat. Management works for them! It's this mindset philosophy of taking "controlling interest" in companies that has allowed these big-time investors to put up staggering returns, year after year ... even in the worst economic climate in our lifetimes. To be clear, these are people that have built their wealth by investing in these types of situations. They have track records that are unmatched in investing, and their bank accounts prove it. You may be thinking that you have the same investments in companies, but have not received the same results. Let's look at the baseline difference.

Simplicity of Purpose. In chapter 6 we talked about seeing into the mind of an investor. Prior to that in the preface we talked about aligning your purpose with that of the investor. While every investor may not be a billionaire, they all think like a billionaires because when they go about building their empires, they are hyper-focused on a specific objective. All their effort and energy is dedicated to pursuing clearly defined purposes. For example:

- Henry Ford wanted to democratize the automobile—to make it available to everyone.
- Bill Gates wanted to put a PC inside every home in America.
- Steve Jobs wanted to put the power of a computer inside a phone (and make it painfully easy to use).

When we look at the whole of these goals, they seem massive, imposing, and yet they can all be stated in a single, easy-to-understand sentence.[7]

Restate your primary goals in a single sentence, and begin to work from there to proliferate all your tasks focuses and benchmark your deliverables.

Simplicity of Plan. Billionaires are not known for having highly detailed, highly elaborate plans. Herb Kelleher, founder of the legendary low-cost people-mover Southwest Airlines, didn't use complicated numbers or ingenious technical secrets to turn the airline industry on its head. His plan for Southwest followed three tenets:

- Get the wheels up and get the wheels down.
- Have fun.
- Embrace being the "low-cost" airline.

These painfully simple tenets are the foundation of the most profitable airline in the history of the aviation industry. Keeping things simple helps all employees—not just key leaders—focus on the activities that will be most impactful to the success of the company.[7]

So why are you asked to create such detailed plans with full financial projections? Understand clearly what is being said, the plan is not eloborate, it is the strategies within the plan that are elaborate. Break out each strategy into its granular detail, but convey your plan in its most simplistic form, so that it is easily digested, understood and agreed upon.

Limit What You Tolerate. Billionaires limit what they tolerate—it sounds callous but it's actually brilliant. Billionaires don't cultivate success from their wants; they extract it from the world by limiting what they'll tolerate.

- They don't tolerate incompetent or unhelpful people.
- They don't tolerate an absence of results.
- They don't tolerate social pressures—they're willing to embrace the isolation, solitude and suffering it takes to build something truly great.

Billionaires are the 1 percent of people who tolerate what 99 percent of us avoid, and generally avoid what 99 percent of us tolerate. They are constantly optimizing their lives. They are asking themselves on a daily basis, Where's the operational drag in my life? What can I get rid of today to make tomorrow better?

Billionaires identify and purge without hesitation—that's why they're creating the greatest outcomes in the world.[7]

Calendly.com is an excellent time management tool that manages your available time schedule. You can dictate the dates and times that you are available. This will eliminate potential time takers. An added benefit is that it will get you to respect your own time, and therefore others will take note and respect your time. Remove excessive notifications from your phone and computer. Only keep notifications for one or two areas such as mail and instant messages. Select a time for your phone to go on 'do not distrub'.

Absolute Reliance on People. Billionaires don't just occasionally lean on other people; they absolutely rely on them to make it through each day. From personal assistants to the members of the board, billionaires cultivate fantastic professional relationships so they can rely on them when they need it most.

Here's why: No single individual could create the leverage and momentum necessary to create billions of dollars in value. It's the billionaire who asks for and offers protection and support, because they know that entrepreneurs accomplish almost nothing alone, and we all move forward faster together.[7]

The reliance on people is not just to get the work completed, it is for the purpose of freeing the mind to its optimum daily usage. Once, all plans, processes and systems have been put in motion, the next logical course is implementation. This is the primary reason for the absolute reliance on people to execute plans, processes and systems.

Absolute Dedication to People. Due, in part, to their reliance on other people, billionaires are also obsessively dedicated to people; this includes customers and investors, but especially employees and their close teams.

This kind of obsession can manifest itself in a variety of ways—some billionaires are obsessed with creating the absolutely perfect product, some are obsessed with spreading success and wealth throughout the world. But it's all ultimately about people.

- Bill Gates, feared early in his career for his fierce temper, learned to become a strong and valued mentor for top leaders at Microsoft.
- Warren Buffett created one of the greatest fortunes and business empires in history, but only after he recognized the need to develop great leaders and keep them close.

And when it comes to the people who create leverage for billionaires, this dedication is absolute and unshakable. The important people in a billionaire's life—from founding partners to their assistants—are always taken care of and usually asked to stay involved in their lives for a long time.[7]

Make no mistake, billionaires are not selfishly going about creating wealth they live their lives in support of others. Most billionaires have well crafted routines in their lives that do not demand the billions they amass, that is why their names always crop up staing how much of their fourtune they give away every year.

Rely on Communications Systems. Everyone knows that for your business to succeed, clear communication is essential. The most successful entreprenuers have trouble communicating. In fact, billionaires, the most successful entrepreneurs, tend to have the greatest difficulty.

But they succeed because they rely exclusively on communications systems, not their own communications skills. All billionaires create ways to accurately track progress, measure results and optimize performance. They understand the importance of being able to gain perspective through context, and they use systematic communication methods that are consistent and reliable.[7]

Communication is regarded as the lifeblood of an organization. You will want to intergrate these objectives into the internal and external communication plans for your business organization:

- Prepartion of organizational plans and policies
- Process flow in exchange between two or more parties
- Timely achievements information of goals
- Organizing of resources and assets
- Maintainance of good industry relationships
- Communication of job satisfaction to employees

Be Intentional With What You Consume. Consumption in the absence of intention is waste. Billionaires are incredibly intentional with their consumption of resources, and no resource is more thoughtfully consumed than information. Typically the information they need is relevant to a highly specific issue or decision. If there isn't a need, billionaires tend to ignore the information.[7]

In chapter 7 we talked in-depth about your pitch, your presentation and what they both should entail. It should now be clear why. The investor's decision is determined from documentable facts. Everything you say, present or provide will be fact-checked for accuracy, doability, and viability to return a profit. I cannot emphasize enough that with each opportuity to be in front of an investor you must be 100% prepared to give them what they are looking for at that very moment.

Think of the overall investor engagement as a 7-Course Dinner.

- Course 1 Amuse-bouche
    - Advocate company speaks on your behalf, to determine interest.
- Course 2 Soup
    - Advocate company sends a Teaser.
- Course 3 Appetizer

- - o Your video.
- Course 4 Salad
  - o You present your plan – 5min.
- Course 5 Main course
  - o You get invited back to give a full 60-minute presentation.
- Course 6 Mignardise
  - o You provide direct answers and information to investors questions.
- Course 7 Coffee, tea or after dinner drink
  - o You meet with Investors to discuss terms & conditions.

HOW MONEY IS MADE

The table below gives you a view of the capitalization risk factor, investment limits, equity/asset position and return on investment based on which entity is capitalizing your project. Some projects utilize combination financing of two or more entity types.

ENTITY	Venture Capital	Banks	Commercial Lenders
RISK FACTOR	100% Risk Investment	0% Risk 100% Financially Qualified Borrower	Up to 65% Risk Investment
INVESTMENT LIMITS	$1K – $Billions+	$1K – Billions+	$10K – Billions+
EQUITY/ASSET POSITION	30% Equity Position	Asset encumbrance upon default	Asset encumbrance upon default
RETURN ON INVESTMENT	3x – 10x Expected ROI	Interest Charged on Loan – up to 30 years	Interest Charged on Loan – up to 30 years

WHAT IS YOUR RELATIONSHIP WITH MONEY?

Financial health or wellness includes: spending money based on your values; having low or reasonable debt; saving and investing money to meet your goals; and having a safety net, such as an emergency fund, insurance and wills.

7 Ways That Money Should Work for You

1. *Pay Attention to It.* Money is like having a child. You would not leave a child to attend to itself. You would nurture it, give it the proper food, care, shelter and direction. When you come to the end of your know-how on child care you would immediately seek help or advice. This is the same systematic process you use with money.

2. *Prioritize It.* Money is a tool. Just as a hammer does not dominate your life, money should also not dominate your life. Money should be seen solely as one of many resources.

3. *Recognize Difference Between Want and Need.* Utilize money to get what you need. Utilize life to get what you want. This clear line of distinction will put money in its proper prospective in your mind. Refer to Way #2.

4. *Keep A Sense of Humor.* Money does and does not grow on trees. For the tree to produce money, you have to do some work.

5. *Don't Manipulate It or Try Power Plays.* Do not take shortcuts to make money, you will just end up having to start again and no amount of money will ever be enough.

6. *Seek to Understand.* In all that you do get an understanding first. Understand the overall purpose of money [see Way #2], and then break that purpose down to your business or project. 99.9% of the time money is not what the business **needs more of**. Make a list of the things, people or ideas the business needs, on that list will you will find answers and directions.

7. *Have Faith in Long Term Vision.* Set your vision long, high and out of reach, such that it only looks like a spec of light. Go variously towards that spec of light with the utmost of passion and determination. You will have given yourself time to prioritize, recognize, understand and build a solid relationship with money.

THE STRENGTH OF MONEY

Relationships

"If you want to go fast, **go alone**. If you want to go far, go together." *African Proverb*

Partnerships

Building the right partnerships will propel business to the next level of impact and influence.

Joint Ventures

Joint Ventures extend your ability to reach markets strategically by adding capital, staff and expertise.

FINANCING YOUR NEXT BILLION$$$

CHAPTER 12

DOMINATE THE DECADE

3 Ways to Dominate the Decade

3 Strategies Business Owners Can Implement Now

Global Fundraising Principles Every Business Must Know

Building A Humanitarian Investment Ecosystem

      As I awakened on the morning of March 2, 2020 still dulled by the news that my daughter Giovanna and her family had set sail on a week-long cruise at a time when the Coronavirus was gaining in the United States, and talk was becoming ever stronger that total shut down of the country was eminent. I was both happy and gravely concerned as I turned on CNN and learned that China's cases had risen to 80,000 and the death toll was rising. Italy and many other countries were quarantining cruise lines at their ports until they were certain no cases of coronavirus existed. March 5th was a milestone Birthday and I understood, but as a mother I was concerned. By God's grace she had a wonderful birthday and they made it back safely without any detainment or delay! Giovanna was in the running to become the next Director of Student Counselors in the Plano High School District in Plano, Texas and she successfully landed that position in April 2020, during the pandemic.

Change, I have spoken about it, I have written about it and I am Co-Founder and Executive Director of the Political Advocacy Organization Women Leading Change Now. While at Laney College in Oakland, California studying Biotechnology I wrote a paper "Standing on the Precipice", where I stated that "man will not change until he is standing on the precipice staring into the abyss, with down as his only solace for what his life has become. It is at that moment that he will change".

The Coronavirus pandemic has set in motion a new definition of change. Until 2020 change had always been gradual, calculated, predictive or a paradigm. The new precedence for change will now be defined not by why we have to change, but by how we change. This is the first time, in our era, that the world has shut down simultaneously, in total agreement that we must shut down and without any discord on how to do it. We just did it together.

The return to 'normal' will obviously be a 'new normal'. We have seen major changes take place during our world wide shut down. 17% of the ozone layer has repaired itself, bees are returning to their natural habitats, the grass is greener, birds are flocking in abundance and the skies are brighter. People are much more cordial and polite to one another. In the United States alone there has been a 60% rise in efforts to raise money, give food, and provide shelter for all citizens. Miami, Florida, USA was murder-free for 7 weeks for first time since 1957. No homicides from Feb. 17 to April 12.[5]

The Coronavirus has most certainly changed the narrative, now you must change your narrative on 'how' you will do business in this new decade. No longer is business as usual sufficient.

3 WAYS TO DOMINATE THE DECADE [DTD]

DTD 1. Develop a 10-Year Strategy

One-Year Incremental Strategies. Here is a tip design year 10 strategy first. Always know your end before you begin. This way you have a defined goal to work towards. Strategy Year 10 can have all your accomplishments wishes, wants and dreams in it. You have 10 years to put make it come to fruition. Designing a one-year strategy is to look in-depth and realistically at what you want to accomplish. See each year as 1/10th of the 10-year goal. Set attainable bench marks. Develop an accountability team to help you stay on track. Freshen up your advisory, working and financial boards. Raise the level of advice expectation that you need. If they are unable or unwilling to give you what you need, you need a new team. If a percentage of income was going to either of these boards they will be happy that you replaced them with people who could move the profit margin up.

Address all of your obstacles in year one. I called a good friend of mine years back and asked what she had been up to lately. She told me she had spent the weekend putting her bills in order. While that was worthwhile to do, I did not understand how that was going to help since she was laid-off at the time. So I asked, what was the purpose. She excitedly answered, "now that I can see everything in front of me, it's not so bad, and I have figured out a way to get back on track and get ahead once my income increases". I was quite impressed, not only had she faced the challenges of determining how to get handle on her finances, but her lexicon had changed. No longer was she saying things would get better once she got a job, instead she said "she had figured out a way to get back on track and get ahead once my income increases". That affirmation alone changed her narrative, and therefore changed her direction. She drew strength and urgency from facing her obstacles, and successfully signed a six-figure contract within 3-weeks.

Obstacles that you may be facing, may be unaddressed customer issues, outdated or non-existing processes, under-capitalization, under-staffed, lack of defined systems, high overhead for office space and the list can go on. Put everything on the list, including back taxes, debts, burn ratios, and anything that is impeding your financial success.

How will I overcome my obstacles? You overcome your obstacles by addressing them head-on. Face them. Get input from your advisors, boards C-Suite Develop implementable plans. Most obstacles are based in poor systems and processes that simply need to be put in place.

In today's technology integrated, app driven, always on world it is no longer an option not to have Better productivity and efficiency with integrated technologies that allow you to organize and share your business data across departments, drastically saving the time and energy needed to look up and verify information. Syncing your systems and sharing the same database means there's no more need to (re-)enter data manually every time, minimizing the window for error.

Become a stronger force in your industry. With the numerous ways to get your message, your voice and your brand in front of your target market it makes it very easy to determine a clear path to get your product to market. Clients and consumers at every level are more educated than any other time in history. This is due in large part to the instant accessibility of the internet, networks, associations, blogs, polls and due diligence.

How then do you show up as an expert in your industry or niche? Entrepreneurs' Guest Writer Kedma Ough who is an Entrepreneur, Inventor, Speaker and SBDC Director gives us 10 Steps to Become an Industry Expert in 12 months. Below is a summation. You can read the full article at https://bit.ly/10-StepIndustryExpert.[6]

1. Purchase the top 10 most popular books on the topic.

Ask for suggestions in industry forums, online or otherwise, or through reference from individuals in your business peer groups.

2. Follow the top industry experts on the topic.

Those with a more public profile will generally have a lot of available information to lead you in your research.

3. Take an industry course.

Rapidly immerse yourself, invest in education seminars or courses. Utilize a site like Udemy that offers quick topic courses on nearly any subject at a very affordable price point.

4. Make connections with others in the domain.

Build a network! The internet can provide a lot of points, and business networking websites, like LinkedIn, can be invaluable when establishing connections. Don't be shy about reaching out to new connections. When you meet with someone for the first time, forward a list of questions in advance to ensure our meeting will be productive and respectful of their time and mine.

5. Join an industry networking association.

This is a wonderful opportunity to meet local experts and create connections for future learning opportunities. Associations offer opportunities to network, attend educational seminars, and receive up-to-date content on specific subject matters. Look in your local area for trade or industry get-togethers on websites like MeetUp. You may be surprised.

6. Attend industry tradeshows or conferences.

National industry tradeshows and conferences afford the opportunity to almost guarantee that top leaders and thinkers in a domain will be under a single roof, and it's a great opportunity to network and participate in training sessions and seminars.

7. Participate in relevant industry advisory groups.

Industry associations exist for most, if not all, industry groups, and there are generally numerous opportunities to support activities that impact and inform industry direction.

8. Listen to podcasts.

An easy way to maximize your time learning about topic is leveraging audio podcasts in your downtime -- perhaps while driving into work in the morning. A lot of podcasts tend to take on a more relaxed, conversational approach to discussing issues and opinions, and make the information sharing more contextual.

9. Stay up to date on the industry news.

Now that news is immediate, leverage the power of readers and viewers to aggregate the information you care about, and find time to review it.

10. Volunteer to support a non-profit organization.

The challenge for a number of not-for-profit groups is not having access to recognized industry experts. Finding a not-for-profit group that both furthers your awareness of aspects of the industry and provides a sense of accomplishment in a lesser-served aspect of an industry can be very rewarding on multiple levels.

Become a podcaster, vlogger. Create a YouTube Channel. Be regular and consistent. It is best to begin with weekly postings and build a following. Guest appear on podcasts, Facebook live, vlogs and all other news/information outlets. Enlist the services of Brand builders to help you create, develop and manage your brand.

DTD 2. Become a Futurist

Look outside of your territory. The world is not flat so your market reach should emulate the world even if you have a local business. Who are you attracting to your business? Who could you be attracting. Develop a future plan to attract new business. Most businesses have a plan to attract new business for today's bottom line. What about the bottom-line in year 3, 5, 7? Make use of the data analytics that you collect on your website, apps, phone surveys. These analytics will provide insight about your clientele's wants, desires and expectations. Do surveys in territories that you currently do not service, but one day would like to add. You will gain insight that can be used in the future product development cycle.

Develop channels of income and influence that are vastly diverse from what you currently do and offer. In the preface of this book I spoke extensively about NASA and the aerospace industry. I can safely say that it takes at least 5K or more different companies collaborating to safely land a rover on Mars. Those 5K plus companies represent at least an additional 10K plus companies that also derive income from the aerospace industry.

Expand your thought process of income and influence to include those that you need to develop, design, manufacture and distribute your product. A simple reciprocal agreement could bring in additional income and clientele.

Years ago, I developed a personal system of investing. In addition to investing with an Investment Banker and an Investment Firm, I wanted to invest myself. I was not sure what I would invest in, so I opened up an account with Ameritrade, I could read current and historical information on companies. But that still did not give me a systematic way of what to invest in. So I developed my own system, by this one single principle. I would use only those things I invested in. I went through my house room by room and wrote down all the major items. Ex. Furniture, fixtures, appliances etc. Then I went back through and listed the material that all items were made from. Ex. Wood, Stone, Plastic etc. The third time I looked at who were the manufacturers and distributors. Now with my three lists I determined that I would invest $1-$5 in each stock. I invest in a different list each week, this gives me time to stay abreast of industry changes and trends. So how is a system like relevant to your business?

A business that you want to increase streams of income and service can be broken down in the same manner in which I went through my home. For example, my venture capital business. I extend my income and business offerings with Virtual Assistants, Affiliates and Collaborative Partners. Many of my collaborative partners provide reciprocal business services that I and my clients utilize such as marketing, accounting, insurance, IT, security, legal services, strategic planning, trusts and wills, investment and fiduciary services.

When you are contemplating adding an additional service find a company that provides that service and collaborate on pricing, services and client referrals. This will greatly reduce your cost to on-board the new service and your go-to-market time will be exponentially reduced. You may also want to consider expanding your business by buying through full or partial acquisition of a company that provides the services you want to offer or are looking to develop.

Become an agile company able to fluidly move from resource to asset. To fully understand how to move from resource to asset we must first understand the difference between the two. "An asset is a resource that is controlled by the person/company from which one can expect to receive future benefits. ... In simple terms, asset creation requires capital. To sum it up, resource is the source of profit. When controlled, resource becomes an asset; and the money used to purchase the asset is the capital".

DTD 3. Give of 90% of yourself and your business

Without thought or contemplation most CEO'S, Presidents, Principals, Owners and Entrepreneurs' give 90% and more daily to their businesses. Now how would that look if it were done intentionally? It would look exceptional! Work in, on and for your business with no expectation of return. The return will present itself. You must see your purpose as greater than yourself. Work for your vision and the mission.

3 STRATEGIES BUSINESS OWNERS CAN IMPLEMENT NOW

There are 3 critical strategies that will position your business for the future?

Strategy 1. Create or strengthen your crisis management plan

1. If the 2020 pandemic caught most businesses with holes in your umbrella, meaning they either did not have a crisis plan or that they needed to put a better crisis management plan in place. The business community realized very quickly that it was a strong crisis management plan that would have kept them operating efficiently during the shut down.

2. Your Crisis Management Plan Must Include a Communications plan, to inform employees who to take direction from. Anticipate that current Leadership may or may not have the ability to communicate. It was very disheartening to see Britain's Prime Minister Boris Johnson fall victim to Coronavirus, but more disheartening was the fact that no successor was named until after his condition became critical, and he was placed in ICU. We thank God that although he was weak, he did recover. Do you have a succession plan currently in place?

3. A critical component to your Crisis Management Plan will be to Add additional security access levels across all IT functions. Data Hackers had field-months of time to comb through tons of unprotected business information during the pandemic. The repercussions will come as a huge expense to small business owners. Many small businesses began early on to suffer through the compromise of consumer data.

Strategy 2. Create or strengthen your online presence

Develop a knowledge based presence, stop selling, start servicing your clientele,

Add TRUE VALUE to your audience, stay away from fluff or empty posts, that simply ask someone to buy your products.

Seek to inform your clients. Clients need information that they can make informed decisions with. Give them the information they need, not the information you want them to have. An educated consumer will always be your best client.

Strategy 3. Create an Expansion Plan

1. Picture this, when you pull your stomach in, your lungs expand. Both systems never contract or expand at the same time. Keeping this picture in mind, the industry is the stomach that is contracting, and the businesses are the lungs that are filling with air and therefore must expand.

2. Opportunities abound in physical health, mental health, medicine, medical supplies communications, spirituality, food services from feeding programs, delivery services, the types of foods we consume, manufacturing, housing, electricity, power, and fuels, the list goes on. What needs did or could you have provided during the pandemic? What needs will your business provide during a future pandemic?

Below is an expansion template that will assist you in positioning your business for future development, as you move forward from design to implementation of your new normal.

Excerpted from "Grow Your Business During Recession" by Yvonne E. Gamble, In The Know EBooks

EXPANSION TEMPLATE

Most expansion plans should feature these 10 key components which are much like a business plan. But the focus is on expansion. Add additional components based on the industry, size and scope of your business.

1. Executive Summary

The executive summary is typically written last, but outlines your whole business plan from start to finish. Keep it simple. Segment your expansion in phases, which will make implementation adaptable to any necessary changes during expansion.

2. Company Description

How does your company stand out from your competitors? Clearly communicate your offerings in a way that will resonate with existing and potential consumers. Who are your target clients and industries? Here is where you outline how your expansion will put you at the forefront of the market. What new innovation are you impacting the market with? Your rationale for expansion should go beyond "to move into new markets and territories". You must have a demonstrable viable change that you will provide.

3. Product and Service Description

Continuing from the company description, outline your products and services in detail. Describe how and why they are important and how they benefit your new consumer base.

4. Marketing Analysis

Outline your market position and how or why companies in your field are growing. Include details such as facts about your industry, the size of your market, and technology associated with business expansion.

5. Marketing Strategy

What strategies will help you sprint to success? Detail advertising, technology, new product innovations, customer experience and touchpoint strategies, collaborations, and ideas for marketing success.

6. Organization and Management

Is your company structure performing to its potential? A well-organized workplace structure can boost morale, efficiency, and benefits for employees and management alike. What role do you play as a CEO, CFO, CMO or marketing director in your business plan? Can inter-departmental teams drive up productivity?

7. Daily Operations

Walk through your day-to-day operations. How have they worked? How will they improve or change as you expand?

8. Financial History

Identify the successful campaigns that have led you to the need for expansion. Detail how these campaigns have transformed your business, as well as how budget cuts or increases have affected your ROI. Demonstrate funds from savings, investments and annuities that will be utilized throughout the expansion period. Investors and lending institutions welcome how you will materially mitigate their investment risk in your expansion.

9. Financial Plan and Projections

Get funded. Your financial plan should outline:

12-month profit and loss projection

three-to-five-year outline on how to retain productivity

cash flow projection

estimated balance sheet of expenditures

cost analysis

10. Appendix

This optional section includes information that helps to build the case for your expansion, including:

valuation

resumes

permits

leases

contracts

brochures

cited industry studies

blueprints

letters of support

Remember: A great plan should be detailed but not convoluted. You want your financiers, clients, and business partners to have a clear understanding of your vision as your business grows, as well as the best methods you will use to achieve your goals.

GLOBAL FUNDRAISING PRINCIPLES EVERY BUSINESS OWNER MUST KNOW

What has helped me down through the years and would be extremely beneficial to business owners is the Association of Fundraising Professionals. One of their funds development series eBooks published in 2013 that stands out to me is Global Fundraising, How The World is Changing the Rules of Philanthropy. It was written by Penelope Cagney and Bernard Ross.[8]

There is a quote that I took "out of this book and put on a wall in my office. "Generosity always finds a way to help those in need" the quote is by Isabella Navarro, former Development Director at the University of Monterrey in Mexico.[8]

To truly understand the global fundraising principles, you must first understand how we got to today. We have been doing global fundraising since the dawn of time from trade routes between Africa, Rome, China, and India and into many other countries and then down into what became the America's.

As our populations and economics grow, so does our social and humanitarian needs grow.

Global Fundraising adheres to **2 guiding principles** that every business owner should seek to incorporate as they embark upon global fundraising.

PRINCIPLE GUIDE 1. Business owners must be proactive and responsive to establishing partnerships and working across borders.

PRINCIPLE GUIDE 2. Business owners have a responsibility and must take an active part in shaping civil society that is inclusive of government, corporate sectors and giving a voice to the voiceless.

BUILDING A HUMANITARIAN INVESTMENT ECOSYSTEM

A Changing Paradigm

> We often think of humanitarian needs as those created by events such as earthquakes, pandemics, famines, or wars. But in fact they extend to the nearly two billion people living under tenuous conditions and those at high risk of crisis—people with very low incomes, people enduring long-term conflict, and people who are newly susceptible to or have been displaced by forces such as climate change. In many of these situations, traditional donation-based assistance via relief organizations is essential, but as crises lengthen and communities become more vulnerable, it is increasingly insufficient. Likewise, development mechanisms cannot fix all the conditions under which such people live and meet all their needs.
>
> New resources are therefore needed to avert or mitigate the next crisis and to build resilience in preparation for those crises that will inevitably occur. Humanitarian investing offers a way to bring in those resources at scale. And the good news is that a growing number of investors want to deploy their

own assets to address these pressing challenges while achieving financial returns. In fact, impact investment assets under management are now estimated at $500 billion globally.

Humanitarian investing focuses on building resilience and self-reliance. Opportunities for impact-driven investors range from pay-as-you-go solar power companies (allowing off-grid communities to buy clean energy only when they need it or can afford it) to loans to refugee entrepreneurs (who tend to pay them back more frequently) to microfinancing for small-holder farmers (enabling them to cope with the effects of climate change). Redirecting just a fraction of the trillions of dollars in the capital markets to investments such as these could go a long way toward strengthening the resilience of fragile communities, releasing far more public, donor, and philanthropic capital for high-risk, high-need purposes than is feasible with private-market investing.

World Economic Forum's New Position on Humanitarian Investment

In a recent white paper from the World Economic Forum (WEF), the World Bank, the International Committee of the Red Cross, and Boston Consulting Group (BCG) provided an opportunity for the right partners to come together to build a humanitarian investment ecosystem by facilitating deals, determining good practices to enable cross-sector collaboration, and setting standards to ensure that help reaches those in greatest need.

The number of existing and potential humanitarian investing projects, as well as their breadth and size, is increasing. An "opportunity platform" developed by BCG and WEF to track the size and nature of the market indicates that there are already thousands of projects in the works that collectively are worth many billions of dollars.

Humanitarian investing operates across different sectors and regions. For example, SunFunder, a solar finance company, works with major debt funders to fill gaps in funding and guidance for SMEs and to help investors diversify their portfolio. With $135 million raised to fund solar projects across sub-Saharan Africa and other regions, SunFunder demonstrates that it is possible to invest in underserved energy markets, often in fragile contexts, while achieving attractive returns.

Meanwhile, InFrontier, a private equity firm that invests in frontier markets, has investments of more than $39 million in Afghanistan and recently opened offices in Pakistan and Uzbekistan. It subjects its investments to due diligence and compliance standards, as would a private equity firm investing in developed markets, adding to this a triple-bottom-line measurement of impact. InFrontier's investors are a mix of public and private investors, such as CDC Group, the Netherlands Development Finance Company, and high-net-worth individuals. With current expected returns of 10% to 15%, the firm has proved that blended financing can establish an equity investment mechanism at a reasonable scale in some of the world's toughest markets.

In cases such as these, different funders and investors play different roles in supporting and developing the humanitarian investment ecosystem. Development finance institutions, among the largest institutional investors working in fragile and conflict-affected areas, can use their access to capital at concessionary rates as a catalyst to bring in other investors and build the humanitarian investment market.[9]

The Future of Investment Continues to Shift

A growing number of large institutional investors today are incorporating environmental, social, and corporate governance (ESG) metrics into their capital allocation and stewardship criteria. This shift toward sustainable finance—which has evolved beyond socially responsible investing to include asset management and ownership—has profound implications for investors and companies alike.

They also recognize that companies that commit to addressing these urgent issues stand to realize greater business opportunities in the future—and thus will achieve higher returns for their long-term shareholders.

Institutional investors that are best poised for the future are those that actively engage with companies through the "power of purpose" instead of simply liquidating their shares and walking away from positions they perceive as questionable in the new climate. Such investors are far better placed to push their holdings in the direction of long-term sustainability through such measures as voting proxies and shareholder resolutions—or by initiating open dialogue with company leaders. Private sector companies and investors that follow this strategy can carve out a far more active role for themselves in the quest for diversity, environmental sustainability, and other important societal goals.

Two trending developments motivate large investors to embrace sustainable finance and to engage directly with corporate executives and boards:

The ubiquity of information about corporate practices. This availability is shining a light on the roles that companies play in shaping the environment and making clear the pivotal role that the private sector will play in finding solutions—or not—to problems such as climate change. Much if not most innovation today occurs within the context of companies, whether startups or incumbents, adopting policies that deliver a positive impact. This is likely to remain the case.

The mounting evidence that addressing ESG issues does not hurt financial performance. In fact, companies that are proactive on issues such as diversity, climate stabilization, and consumer responsiveness can deliver substantial financial rewards.

THE BUSINESS CASE FOR COMPANIES TO ENGAGE IN HUMANITARIAN RESPONSE

In Nov 2017 OCHA The United Nations Office of Humanitarian Affairs published "The business case: A Study of Private Sector Engagement in Humanitarian Action". Here are some of their findings that do support businesses integrating humanitarian response into their business modality.

While social and ethical responsibility is usually cited as the main reason motivating private sector companies to engage in humanitarian response, this engagement can also create clear business opportunities, and can also benefit companies' bottom line.

In recent years, humanitarian partnerships involving private sector companies are on the rise, with initiatives emerging in the mega-typhoon in the Philippines, the earthquake in Haiti, the conflicts in Syria and Yemen and the Ebola outbreak in West Africa. These partnerships have been forged around different areas including communications technology, logistics, health, education, shelter, water, sanitation and hygiene (WASH), cash transfers, leadership training and the provision of technical support in crises.

Based on extensive surveys and more than 50 interviews with business representatives, the study looked at why and how the private sector engages in humanitarian action, unpacking the "business case" for collaboration between private companies and humanitarian organizations.

While corporate social responsibility is "first and foremost the opportunity to help the most vulnerable communities to become more resilient," as one survey respondent said – a significant 70 per cent of respondents added that the expected return on investment was a crucial factor in deciding whether to pursue a partnership.

The study identified four concrete drivers of private sector engagement in humanitarian action:

1. To develop commercial opportunities by accessing and testing new markets.

2. To reduce business risk and mitigate loss by protecting the consumer base.
3. To build relationships with other businesses, international organizations and governments.
4. To enhance business assets such as the company's reputation or staff skills and motivation: "By engaging in humanitarian action, companies can test and evaluate internal standard operating procedures and instruments and have the chance to train employees under extreme circumstances," one respondent explained.

The study also looked at four models of engagement that can add concrete value for businesses in a partnership:

1. Businesses with products or services relevant to a humanitarian response interested in developing their business assets, innovation or accessing new markets.
2. Businesses operating in areas potentially affected by humanitarian crises protecting their staff, infrastructures, and customers before, during and after humanitarian crises.
3. Businesses providing pro bono products or services to improve the internal operations of humanitarian organizations or the humanitarian system as a whole.
4. Businesses, their staff and their customers, making financial contributions in an effective and impactful way through aid organizations or directly to affected people.

How to organically integrate humanitarian services in your business model

During the 2020 Pandemic across the globe businesses were called into action from farmers, grocers, ppe suppliers, medical device companies, first responder emergency companies, security organizations from personal security to internet security. These and many more became deemed 'essential'. New emerging companies like UBERMED, blood, plasma and organ transport company and MOBIMED PPE Supplier found themselves and their businesses propelled into the forefront as service providers. Restaurateurs who initially thought they would be far left behind, pivoted immediately becoming curb side locations with the addition of drive through lanes to accommodate pick-ups from UberEats, GrubHub and Lift.

New upstart millennial companies like Momentum Emani, headed by my youngest daughter Erika Gamble, found themselves doing double duty with website development and having to also provide internet security services.

With menus changed, service increased exponentially and more jobs created, most restaurants saw extended rather than shortened hours. Velma Jean's Chicken & Waffles Southern Food and BBQ, in Tylertown, Mississippi found itself giving free meals to the less fortunate in the community it served. Its' efforts did not go unnoticed by the local population and donations and client's poured in as it was the only restaurant open. In May 2020 they were able to move one of their workers who graduated college virtually in May 2020 up to General Manager.

Small business can play a big role in humanitarian crises beyond financial

The 125 million people in need of humanitarian assistance around the world in the international community are increasingly unable to finance their growing needs.

The problem is likely to get worse before it gets better. The UN raised more money ($24.5 billion) for humanitarian assistance in 2014 than in any year on record while still recording its biggest-ever shortfall in humanitarian financing, with only 62% of global needs covered. In other words, the growth in costs is outpacing the ability of the humanitarian system to raise more funds.[10]

The world's needs are expanding so much faster than its generosity? Most stakeholders agree that one of the biggest drivers of the shortfall is the changing nature of humanitarian crises themselves. Historically, the cost of responding to humanitarian crises was split equally between natural disasters and human conflict. Today, 80% of humanitarian needs are caused by conflict - often with complex political dimensions - with most being recurrent or protracted crises. The average length of conflict-related displacement now reportedly stands at 17 years. These trends are putting sustained pressure on a humanitarian system that was designed for short-term emergencies.[10]

Another striking aspect of the funding crisis is that the private sector is not doing its share. A shockingly low 4.8% of global humanitarian appeals were met by private sector donors in 2014. There are reasons for this, including the trust deficit that has emerged between the private and humanitarian sectors, and the historical tendency of humanitarian agencies and non-governmental organizations to treat the private sector as a checkbook rather than a true partner. However, it must be remedied if the international community is to make better use of the full range of assets at its disposal.[10]

Encouragingly, some changes are already underway. Today, there is a growing willingness in the humanitarian sector to make better use of the private sector's skills, capabilities and diverse networks rather than just seek financial donations. For example, the World Food Programme has partnered with MasterCard since 2012 to streamline aid distribution with the use of electronic payments technology. The expertise of logistics and insurance companies is being tapped to develop innovative solutions to some of the humanitarian sector's key operational challenges. Discussions are also underway with Islamic financial institutions about creating more innovative sharia-compliant social finance bonds dedicated to addressing urgent humanitarian needs.[10]

The Future of Humanitarian Aid Must Change to be Sufficient

The world's current humanitarian aid architecture is growing outdated. Relief programs are most effective when they are integrated, locally owned, and demand driven. But humanitarian action in the 21st century remains constrained by a 20th-century aid model: siloed, supply driven, and centered on the individual mandates and sectors of major international aid agencies.[11]

Humanitarian international aid agencies will find themselves giving up their control over areas of needs and allow for true aid resource flow and restoration of affected communities. The agencies must move away from the always degenerated and needed model to one that creates sustainable independent ecosystems of growth. It is at this intersection that the business community will ensue its greatest contribution.

Practical steps toward people-driven aid. The humanitarian sector has long affirmed that the people we serve must be at the center of response and have meaningful input on the decisions that affect their lives. Living up to the aspiration of people-driven humanitarian action will require uncomfortable—but overdue—changes to the humanitarian system's incentive structures and power dynamics.[11]

New financing models: Traditional donor practices tend to incentivize siloed programming rather than collective impact. As trends like multipurpose cash and joint needs assessments will better push the humanitarian system toward more integrated delivery.[11]

Area-based coordination: The existing cluster coordination system furnishes the building blocks of humanitarian program strategy, response planning, and (through cluster lead agencies) financing. Center for Global Development has presented emerging ideas on how area-based coordination models—which are geographically targeted, explicitly multisectoral, and can engage the affected population through participatory design—could offset many of the shortcomings inherent in the cluster-based coordination model.[11]

FINANCING YOUR NEXT BILLION$$$

REFERENCES

1. "Data Driven Venture Capital", Pat Grady Partner Sequoia Capital 12/18/2018 pg. 6 https://www.cbinsights.com/
2. Chapter 2 – My Team
"CORPORATE FINANCE & ACCOUNTING FINANCIAL STATEMENTS Shareholder" REVIEWED BY ADAM HAYES
Updated Apr 8, 2019
https://www.investopedia.com/terms/s/shareholder.asp
3. Jul 14, 2018, 3:40 am EST, he 7 Best Presentation Software Tools for Entrepreneurs
Alejandro Cremades Former Contributor Entrepreneurs, Author of The Art of Startup Fundraising & Serial Entrepreneur, March 4, 2020,
https://www.forbes.com/sites/alejandrocremades/2018/07/14/the-7-best-presentation-software-tools-for-entrepreneurs/#4aa336fa2eac
4. The Dragons' Den Guide to Investor-Ready Business Plans 12/20/2018. Pg 48 By John Vyge
https://books.google.com/books?id=gTGwCgAAQBAJ&pg=PA49&lpg=PA49&dq=investor+customer+interview&source=bl&ots=uZVc4jY0Fg&sig=Wvc6ZvMHb3ZAf-Wur2_wsvAAt5s&hl=en&sa=X&ved=2ahUKEwjO4amI_K7fAhWjdN8KHbfhAvoQ6AEwBnoECAAQAQ#v=onepage&q=investor%20
5. Miami was murder-free for 7 weeks for first time since 1957. No homicides from Feb. 17 to April 12. May 23, 2020
https://www.wptv.com/news/state/miami-dade/miami-was-murder-free-for-7-weeks-for-first-time-since-1957
6. 10 Steps to Become an Industry Expert in the Next 12 Months Kedma Ough, Guest Writer, Entrepreneur, Inventor, Speaker; SBDC Director. May 23, 2020. https://www.entrepreneur.com/article/290867
7. The 10 Principles of Self-Made Billionaires by Alex Charfen, May 30, 2016.
https://www.success.com/the-10-principles-of-self-made-billionaires/

8. Global Fundraising: How the World is Changing the Rules of Philanthropy 1st Edition by Penelope Cagney (Author), Bernard Ross (Author) https://www.amazon.com/Global-Fundraising-World-Changing-Philanthropy/dp/1118370708
9. Building Resilience Through Humanitarian Investing. January 23, 2020 By Douglas Beal, Carl Brinton, and David Young. May 24, 2020 https://www.bcg.com/publications/2020/building-resilience-through-humanitarian-investing.aspx
10. How small business can play a big role in humanitarian crises, Jan 13, 2017 By Badr JafarChief Executive Officer, Crescent Enterprises, https://www.weforum.org/agenda/2017/01/how-small-business-can-play-a-big-role-in-humanitarian-crises/
11. Five Takeaways on the Future of Humanitarian Reform, Jeremy Konyndyk, August 7, 2019, https://reliefweb.int/report/world/five-takeaways-future-humanitarian-reform

ABOUT THE AUTHOR

Yvonne E Gamble has 35+ years in the Financial Industry beginning as a Million+ Dollar Account Representative with American National bank to now CEO of SanPete Financial Group, a venture capital firm that raises between $5M and $120B for startups. growing and expanding companies. Gamble is determined to help you increase your knowledge and financial prowess, optimize your business offerings, and differentiate your brand by passing on her cumulative knowledge. She vigilantly stays on top of the latest in venture capital funding, financial trends and business marketing, bringing you the top insights with expert commentary, through her "In The Know" EBooks, as a Keynote Speaker or in one of her Guest Authoring Thrive Global commentary articles.

www.ingramcontent.com/pod-product-compliance
Lightning Source LLC
Chambersburg PA
CBHW021447210526
45463CB00002B/674